Better Homes and

KITCHEN
MAKEOVER & PROJECT BOOK

Catherine Cumming

MURDOCH BOOKS®
Sydney • London • Vancouver • New York

Contents

Buying a new kitchen is without doubt an enjoyable and exciting venture. It can, however, be expensive and there are other, cheaper ways to transform the kitchen you already have. Paint is inexpensive and offers you an immediate way to update not only your walls but your floors, furniture and accessories too. Today's demand for colour has led to a huge growth in the range of paint colours available. There are literally hundreds of colours to choose from in a number of finishes suitable for various surfaces.

This book should be used as a practical guide to selecting paints and colours for your kitchen. Discussion on colour theory will help you to choose and use colour in the home. Practical advice on paint products and their suitability is combined with inspirational examples showing the use of colour and its effect. The selection of projects undertaken here can all be adapted to suit your own ideas, for your own kitchen.

In this book, the same kitchen has been given six makeovers using a range of different colour schemes and styles. Although the kitchen has remained the same, the floor and the splashback have been changed to different materials, and the door knobs have been changed each time. The colour schemes vary from a bright and sunny Caribbean theme, to the warm and earthy colours of Morocco. These countries inspired certain colour tones and combinations, but there are many others to choose from. The colours of the neutral kitchen create a soft and restful atmosphere, whereas the 1950s colour scheme is

more lively and exciting. If you possess stainless steel appliances and cooking utensils you may be inspired by the lime green kitchen, or try your own choice of colour with the same paint effects. Blue is a colour that is often associated with country kitchens—the blue kitchen featured in this book has been distressed with crackling paint effects. I hope you can see how very different one kitchen can appear in a different colour, using a different paint effect.

All the paint effects and techniques shown throughout this book can be used in many different colours and styles. Experiment first and try out your ideas on cardboard, lining paper or on off-cuts of wood. Keep your test boards in the kitchen for a few days, see how they change throughout the day in the different light levels and take your time deciding if you like them there —or not!

In these makeovers colour is not only employed in paint but also in other elements, such as fabric in the

curtain making project, or tiles on the mosaic table. The individual projects allow as much or as little of that particular look to be re-created. With in-depth information on preparation and basic techniques, an absolute beginner to home decoration can have the confidence to put these ideas into practice. Everything you need to know to get started is contained within these projects.

The kitchen is the heart of the home, so do not overlook the importance of creating a happy and joyful environment. Painted kitchens can be re-painted again and again over the years as your choice of colours changes. There is no excuse for putting up with a decor you don't enjoy! There are many elements to consider when decorating your kitchen but there are no right or wrong colours to use. There is a great delight to be had in painting and enjoying colours—we need colour like we need light. So take responsibility for your kitchen now and make it a room to enjoy!

Using Colour in Your Kitchen

Every kitchen, like every person, has its own unique character. When choosing clothes for a person, there are many different aspects to consider—the size, the shape, the natural colouring and the personality. To make the best choice for your kitchen, consider carefully all the different aspects involved.

KITCHEN LIGHTING

The first consideration may be that of lighting; good natural daylight can be quite a luxury in many city flats and houses. If you are more dependent on artificial lighting, remember that many colours, especially yellows, change considerably in this type of light. Some light bulbs cast a blue hue, giving yellow a cooler, greeny appearance. Other warmer-coloured bulbs project a yellower golden light. If you are going to change the lighting in your kitchen, make sure you do so before finally deciding on a particular colour for your decorating scheme. You could end up with something completely different from what you had planned!

While you are actually painting your kitchen, switch the lights on and off occasionally to check the effect and always try to paint in natural daylight when you can. It is helpful to test your colour first on an odd scrap of wood or hardboard, then leave it in the room for a

Two of these kitchens
illustrate using opposite
colours (top left and
bottom right). Orange
and blue are opposite
colours and so contrast
and complement one
another dramatically. In
contrast, the colours in
the kitchen bottom left
are all from the same
area of the colour wheel
and therefore blend
more quietly. Blue and
white is a traditional
colour combination.

7

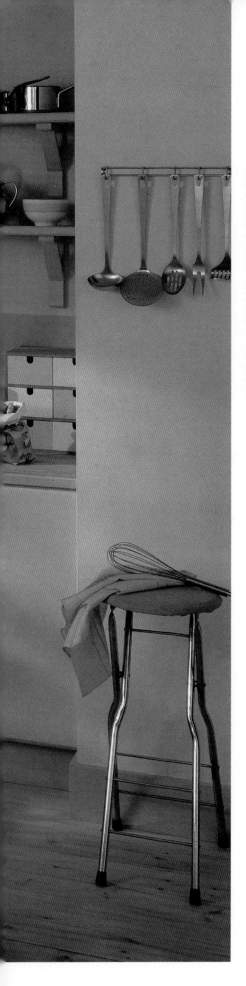

few days. Look at it at different times of the day and notice if and how it changes. It is also helpful to leave a sample of the wall colour next to it. See how these colours sit together and decide, over a few days, whether you grow to like this combination. Try to paint as large a sample board as you can. Better still, try to paint large areas of the colour on the wall. If this is in water-based paint, it can of course be painted over again quickly and easily.

C O L O U R S   O N   A   C O L O U R   C H A R T

When choosing colours from the little colour cards you buy in shops it can be suddenly daunting to see the same colour in all its glory on a whole wall. The full impact can prove too strong. The lighting in paint shops is often

quite different from the lighting in your home. Take the paint charts out of the shop, and look at them on the street in natural daylight.

Try to test a colour in as large an area as possible. Although not available at many paint shops, some outlets do supply small tester pots of matt water-based paint—an inexpensive and practical way of testing colours—especially those that might look very similar on a colour chart but clearly different on a wall.

If it is not possible to paint samples directly on to your wall, paint on to lining paper. Cut pieces of this to size and hold them up to the wall. Sometimes four walls painted in exactly the same colour can look quite different throughout the day, and quite different from each other.

F U N C T I O N A L   C O N S I D E R A T I O N S

Nowadays, many people use the kitchen as a dining room too. If the two functions of your kitchen are in one and the same area, you could paint different elements such as the table and chairs to match or complement the units. In the blue kitchen, for example, the table and chairs were painted in the darkest cream colour used on the walls. Then a simple painted flower pattern was added using the same blue as used for the kitchen. This is a very easy method of bringing together different elements.

If the kitchen and dining area are separate, you could connect them through colour. You could, for example, carry the kitchen wall colour through to the dining area and treat it in a different way. If it is a colourwash, you could gently alter the tone, making it softer and warmer as you approach the dining area. Or, you could keep the same colour but add a painted frieze or border as you leave the kitchen area. Choose something from the same theme, such as the squares from the neutral kitchen, or the pattern from the Moroccan kitchen.

SIZE AND SPACE

Light and cool colours project a feeling of space. Cool colours, such as soft blues and greens, recede: the walls appear further away and the space appears larger. The opposite effect is achieved with warmer colours, such as yellow, red and orange. The walls appear to advance towards you and the space seems smaller. Darker colours make a room look smaller, while lighter colours create space and light.

Consider the size of your kitchen in terms of the impact of your chosen colours. The 1950s kitchen, for example, may be too lively and the colours too strong in a very small area. The neutral kitchen would bring a feeling of space and light into a small area. The Moroccan kitchen would make a small space look smaller

but at the same time more cosy and intimate. Think about the effects you would like to achieve in your given space. If you have a small kitchen, don't automatically try to make it look bigger. Warm and intimate colours might be much more suitable.

KITCHEN LAYOUT

Consider the existing layout of your kitchen. Do you want to bring a disjointed layout together with the colours you use or do you want to separate certain areas through colour? In the lime green kitchen, for example, different tones of lime green were used on the walls. The back wall was a deeper shade of lime green, and the two adjacent walls were a lighter shade. Using different strengths of a particular wall colour has the effect of bringing

SOOTHING
BLUE

There is an enormous range in the colour blue. It is a primary colour and sits between green and red on the colour wheel. Green blues, such as aqua and turquoise, tend to be cooler than the redder blues, such as lavender. The blue stool is painted with a middle blue with no green or red added, just black and white to create different tints and shades.

certain walls forward and taking others back. In a long thin room, for example, you might want to use darker tones on the walls furthest away to bring them into the room, and lighter tones on the walls closest together so they appear further apart.

When painting blocks of colour, as in the 1950s kitchen, you might want to use this effect to link in and balance different elements of your kitchen. In this makeover, a separate cupboard was painted in the same style to make this part of the central kitchen. You could do the same with doors, windows, tables, chairs or other pieces of furniture.

Colour can also add weight to certain items. Dark warm colours can add weight to a surface, giving a more solid and fixed appearance. The opposite effect is achieved with light cool colours. The colourwashing technique in the Caribbean kitchen (see page 83), for example, could be graduated to extend to the height of a wall. If the wash is darker on the lower areas of the wall and you gradually lighten the colour the higher up you paint, it will have the effect of lifting the wall, raising the height of the ceiling and the length of the wall.

CONCEALING UGLY FEATURES

Most kitchens have their fair share of elements you wish you could hide. These may include pipes and radiators and boxed-in taps. Try to paint as many of these as possible to lose them into the wall, skirting board or door. Do remember, though, to use the correct type of paint on different surfaces. A paint finish on hot pipes will flake off in no time, so do use an appropriate solvent-based paint to blend these into the wall or the units. Any pipes, taps or boxes on the wall or skirting board can also be painted. Treat radiators in the same way. If they are to be painted the same colour as the wall (the best way to lose them if you have no radiator cover or box) remember not to use water-based paint as it will crack or flake off. Use a solvent-based paint to match as best you can. Try to avoid using solvent-based glazes or varnish on radiators. As the radiators heat up, the linseed oil in glaze and oil-based varnish will discolour and cause the radiator to stand out yet again! This is especially evident in blue glazes that turn noticeably green. Any radiator boxes and shelves will also be affected by the heat and suffer in the same way.

HIGHLIGHTING ATTRACTIVE FEATURES

There may be some elements of your kitchen that you choose to make a feature of through your use of colour. You may have a cornice or a ceiling rose, for example. These could be brought

BRILLIANT
RED

Red appears the strongest, most aggressive colour of the primaries. It excites and enlivens and it is thought to induce conversation, so the type of red should be well chosen! On the colour wheel, red sits between violet and orange. On the violet side red becomes deep crimson, heavy and majestic, while on the orange side red becomes fierce and fiery.

S U M M E R Y

VIOLET

Violet is a secondary colour formed by mixing red and blue, and can range from pinky-lilac to lavender. It can be a warm and gentle colour, but in its darker and redder forms it may appear a little heavy. Used in its purest and softest forms, however, it can both soothe and uplift, as evident in beautiful summer flowers.

out by washing colour over them using the same method as colour-washing with scumble glaze (see page 83). There were no cornices to deal with in these six kitchens, but you need not have a fancy cornice to treat this way—a simple curved cornice can be lightly washed and gently brought into the walls.

Do not neglect the skirting boards either. In all of the six kitchen treatments in the book, the skirting board was brought into the kitchen by treating it in the same way as the doors.

LINKING COLOURS
The two major existing features to consider in any kitchen are the worktop and the floor. Where possible, do try to connect these colours in some way to the colours you choose for your kitchen scheme. For example, a white worktop could be balanced with a white sink, white appliances, and a white base coat showing through a colourwashed wall. Mottled and wooden worktops are easiest to deal with as they offer many different shades to pick out and use in the walls, or the unit doors. This is, of course, not always necessary—it just makes for a gentler, softer connection.

Wooden floors, like wooden worktops, are easier to pick colours from as there are often many different colours in the wood itself, especially in pale wood. Wooden floors can easily be painted—in the 1950s kitchen the floor was painted grey to match the skirting and frame of the kitchen. There are many products available to make floor painting as easy as possible; acrylic floor paint, linoleum paint and tile paint are now available and easy to use.

Window blinds and curtain fabric are also very important influences for colour. The 1950s kitchen was painted entirely around the curtain fabric. When you are planning your decorating scheme, try to take into account all the different elements in your kitchen before painting, as it is easier to adapt the paint colour to work with what you have than the other way around.

CEILING COLOUR

Most kitchen ceilings are white. It is clean, fresh and bright and usually works well in most kitchens. Kitchens are, after all, working areas and a white ceiling allows the light to reflect clearly on to the work surfaces, making it much brighter and easier to work. Even the fairly dark Moroccan kitchen retained a white ceiling for this reason.

Off-white, creamy colours may work better for your particular colour scheme, though, and will not affect the light too much; they could in fact add a little more warmth and intimacy to the room. A darker warmer colour on

CITRUS
YELLOW

Yellow is a vibrant primary colour, placed between green and orange on the colour wheel. In its green form yellow becomes limey and acid, fresh and sharp. In its orange form it becomes warm and golden. Yellow is the colour closest to sunlight and in its purest form creates a special glow —like gold—joyous and lively.

R E F R E S H I N G

GREEN

Green is the colour formed by mixing blue and yellow. In its yellow form it can take on a striking character that is a dazzlingly fresh and cool lime green. In its blue form, sea green, it can be a cool, soft and yet vibrant colour. Green is often mixed to an earthy tone to simulate the colours of foliage. It is the colour most associated with nature, and so promotes a healthy, restful feeling of comfort.

the ceiling will advance towards you so the ceiling appears to be lower than it is. A lighter cooler-coloured ceiling will have the opposite effect, so the ceiling will appear higher.

U S I N G   P A T T E R N

Pattern can enhance and echo various shapes in a room. In the neutral kitchen a very simple pattern along the side edge of a wall was used. The square shape was taken directly from the size, shape and colouring of the splashback ceramic tile.

Inspiration for patterns can be sought in many ways. Try looking at pattern source books, old tiles or pictures and postcards of patterns. The pattern used in the Moroccan kitchen was taken from a floor tile.

You can use paint and colour to soften patterns. If you find your pattern looks too strong, rub it down lightly with sandpaper. You could age the pattern further by using a brown wash (see the Caribbean kitchen doors, page 84). This will soften the overall effect of a pattern. Pattern on a mottled background has a gentler effect, and the contrast is already softened. The patterns in both the neutral and the Moroccan kitchens were painted on to a mottled base.

Pattern is usually used quite sparingly in kitchens. They are busy spaces with different heights and shapes to contend with.

Worktops and cupboards become full with patterned cups and crockery, food packets, and so on, all of which have contrasting colours. So pattern in the kitchen should be used carefully.

PSYCHOLOGICAL IMPACT OF COLOUR

The most important consideration in choosing colour for your kitchen is the effect it has on you and your mood. There are basic loose guidelines about the psychological impact of colour. Certain colours excite and enliven (for example, red and orange), some uplift (like golden yellow) while others calm and relax (such as blue).

Green is said to be a soothing colour, evoking the natural surroundings, and is a good colour for a kitchen that leads out to the garden. This is an example but also a generalization, as one colour can receive many different responses. Everyone has their own personal associations with specific colours and reactions are subjective. Primarily you need to choose colours you enjoy. Consider also whether you want a kitchen to relax in, like the neutral kitchen or the blue kitchen, or whether you want one to promote alertness, activity and creativity, like the vibrant 1950s kitchen, or if you prefer the warm, cosy feeling of the Moroccan-style kitchen. The only rule is to enjoy the effects you create.

WARMING

ORANGE

Orange is made from yellow and red. It is a powerful and splendid colour, the colour of log fires and sunsets. In its yellow form orange is light and lively; in its redder version it becomes richer, more fierce and flame like. Orange in decoration is often toned down with paler colours to form apricot tones, or mixed with browns to form burnt ochres and warm rustic terracottas. It is a warming colour, rich and majestic.

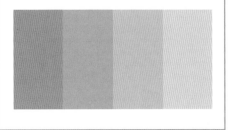

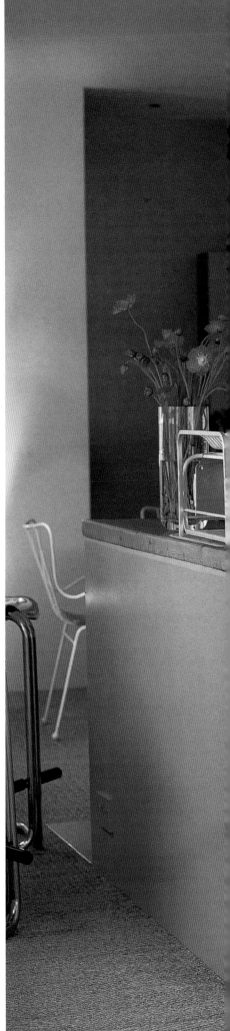

Paint Products

The selection of paints, varnishes and decorating products that are available can be quite confusing for a keen amateur. These pages will help you through the maze of products and guide you to the correct selection for the project you are undertaking and the surfaces on which you intend to apply it.

Paint is coloured pigment suspended in a medium which makes it spreadable and gives it an acceptable drying time. Paint also contains the relevant chemicals to ensure that it does not rub off easily and that the colour will not fade too much. It can be helpful to understand how paint is manufactured. There are two main processes involved; one for water-based paints and one for oil-based paints.

All of the projects in this book have used water-based products. If you do use water-based paint on kitchen units, make sure they are properly prepared and primed so this paint will adhere (see page 26).

Other products mentioned here are alternatives.

WATER-BASED PAINTS

Water-based paints are commonly known as acrylic paints. They are water soluble and are generally made by pushing ground pigment (colour in its purest form) into a solution of water and polyvinyl acetate (PVA) resin. PVA is a type of plastic. The pigment is forced into the resin and water at such high speed that it breaks up and disperses evenly. When you apply a PVA paint to your walls you are effectively applying a skin of coloured plastic and water. The water evaporates and you are left with an even coating of coloured plastic. The greater the shine on the PVA paint, the higher the ratio of plastic to water.

OIL-BASED PAINTS

Oil-based paints, such as satin and gloss, are more complicated to make. Oil-based paint is made by first making a binder, which is a mixture of alcohol and linseed oil. To this are added some thinners (mineral turpentine) and ground white pigment, and this is then mixed. The pigment does not break up and disperse during this process so the mixture is now ground in a mill to ensure that an evenly whitened paint base results. Finally, some more thinners are added, along with a chemical drier and some stainers. The product goes through a staining process before it is officially called paint. You may be familiar with paint base; this is the product to which the paint stores add stainers to colour the paint to your requirements. So, when you apply oil-based paint you are covering your surface with coloured oils. As it contains all these chemicals you will understand why oil-based paint smells so powerfully.

UNDERCOAT

Undercoat can be either water or oil based. It is a thin surface preparation and is used to seal walls and wood-work prior to painting the top coat. Undercoat has a matt finish.

SEMI GLOSS PAINT

Oil-based, semi gloss, or satinwood paint has a good satin shine to it and usually a greater intensity and lustre of colour. It has a tough finish, and is used mainly for woodwork. In its oil-based form it has an offensive smell; it is recommended that you work in a well-ventilated area to prevent inhalation of the fumes. Oil-based paints take a longer time to dry than water-based paints. Semi gloss paint with a water base dries quicker, but with not so fine a finish.

LOW SHEEN PAINT

Low sheen paint is much the same as matt but easier to clean and has a slight shine to it. For some paint techniques your base must have a slight shine so this paint is recommended in place of matt finishes. All the projects in this book have been done in matt, on matt. There are now washable paints available which can overcome the difficulties of keeping a matt surface look-ing like new.

PRIMER

Primer can be either water or oil based. It is most often used on bare wood to seal the surface and prevent the wood from swelling when the undercoat and top coat are applied. Primer is also used on metal for protection against corrosion and rust.

GLOSS PAINT

Gloss paint is traditionally oil based and has a full gleam to it. It is more difficult to apply and should be brushed over an undercoated surface in two coats using a good-quality brush. Over time, the shine of the gloss may reduce and it will need to be re-painted. Water-based gloss is also available but, as with semi gloss, does not have such a fine finish.

TEXTURE PAINT

Texture paints are designed to give texture and protection to smooth exterior concrete, cement renderings, brick and fibrous cement sheeting. The degree of texture varies con-siderably according to the type of pigment or aggregate used in the coating. This type of finish can be used on both domestic and commercial buildings.

FLUORESCENT PAINT

Fluorescent paint is brilliantly coloured and highly visible even in poor light. These paints are only efficient when applied over white ground colour. They have poor dura-bility and should be protected with a coat of clear finish.

MATT (OR FLAT) PAINT

Matt paint is very practical and inexpensive for covering large areas quickly. As it is water based, it does not have an offensive smell and has no shine at all. Matt paints can be difficult to wash if they become dirty but any small areas can be touched up very easily.

WOODSTAIN

This is most often used for colouring untreated or bare wood. It can be either water or spirit based. Woodstain soaks deep into the grain of the wood but is semi transparent so that the original grain will still show through. Apply it in generous quantities and wipe the surface with a soft cloth once it is dry. Woodstain does not actually protect raw wood and therefore you must varnish or wax the surface after colouring it in order to protect it.

VARNISH

Most varnish comes through the initial production stages looking like clear gloss. Silicon powders are added to make a satin or matt finish. These powders settle in the can so it is imperative that you stir the varnish well both before and regularly during use. Generally, the thinner the varnish, the easier it is to apply and the better the quality of your finished work will be. All oil-based varnish tends to yellow and this is very noticeable on pale surfaces. You can stain varnish very easily for your own use by stirring in some diluted artist's colours. Use oil colours for polyurethane varnishes and acrylics for water-based varnishes.

Acrylic-based varnish does not yellow, it dries quickly and does not smell. Use oil-based varnish on oil finishes and acrylic varnish on water-based paint, such as acrylic scumble glaze.

WAX

Wax offers an easy way to bring some protection and sheen to wood. Wax will nourish and protect most wooden surfaces and can be repaired and touched up easily. Beeswax is still one of the best wood polishes (and also smells very pleasant). All you need to do is apply the wax just like a floor polish, leave it to dry and then buff with a soft cloth. Re-apply wax from time to time as the sheen dulls.

Waxes containing colourants are also available; these will stain the wood as you go. You may need to carry out several applications of coloured wax before you achieve the colour shown on the can. For large areas, such as a wooden floor, you will need to hire a professional buffing machine.

SCUMBLE GLAZE

Scumble glaze is a transparent medium which can be coloured for use in creating special paint effects. In simple terms, it makes the colour slippery and moveable. The glaze is applied with a brush or roller and manipulated with rags, brushes, plastic or anything you like. When the desired effect is achieved, the glaze is left to dry. It is then usually varnished for protection and durability.

Scumble glaze is available in oil- or water-based forms; the oil-based glaze has more lustre and depth to it and takes longer to dry than acrylic-based glaze. For some particular finishes, you must take care to complete an entire section in one rapid session and if the glaze begins to dry at the edges you will see a significant 'watermark' where the overlaps are. Stop only in the corners of a wall having brought the glazed section to a neat finish.

ENAMEL AND CRAFT PAINTS

These paints are sold in small quantities and are useful for small jobs, detailing and murals. Their colours are very intense. Most enamels do not need to be protected with varnish and will keep their colour for years. Craft paints, on the other hand, may be water based and might resist a surface which has been prepared in oils. Always buy the best craft paint you can afford. Cheap craft paint may not be made with the best pigments and the colour can fade rapidly.

ARTIST'S OIL CRAYONS

These crayons are just like children's wax crayons except that they are oil based. They can be used for little touching-up jobs and for drawing fine lines where a paintbrush may be too bold, heavy or difficult to handle. An oil crayon can be sharpened to a point, and the colour can also be thinned or smudged with the aid of a little mineral turpentine.

UNIVERSAL STAINERS

This is a coloured stain liquid form which can be added to water-based or oil-based paints in order to adjust the colour. It is available in traditional artist's colours. Try raw umber for 'dirtying' a colour.

PURE PIGMENT

Sold in powder form by art shops, pure pigment is the base of all the traditional colours on an artist's palette. The colour is the most intense available and it can be mixed into either oil- or water-based products. It is expensive but you do not need to use much at a time.

LINSEED OIL

Linseed oil can be used to make your own transparent paints by mixing with artist's oil paints or pure pigments, a dash of mineral turpentine and, very importantly, a few drops of driers. Use refined or boiled linseed oil to minimize the yellowing effect. Linseed oil does not dry without chemical help from driers.

DRIERS

These chemical additives can be added to oil paints to speed up the drying time. Be careful not to add too much; one teaspoon is sufficient for 1 litre (32 fl oz) of oil-based paint. Any more than this may affect the shine of the paint, and make it appear powdery.

WHITING

This is a white powder, made from chalk, which can be added to home-made linseed oil paint in order to make it less transparent. Mix the oil into the powder a little at a time to avoid lumps, rather than putting powder into the paint. Thin with turpentine, mineral turpentine or water, depending on the medium of your paint.

Troubleshooting

THE COLOUR IS WRONG

If you are not happy with the colour you have applied, repainting the whole room is not the only solution to this problem! If the colour you have applied is fairly pale or light, consider glazing over it using a simple paint technique such as colourwashing. Your base colour will be toned down by this but will still glow through the transparent glaze.

If the colour looks too dark try washing or sponging one or two lighter colours on top. Your base colour will show through but the whole effect will become lighter and mottled. If you are using two or more colours for sponging, use the lightest colour last.

THE SHEEN IS WRONG

The acrylic paint you have used either does not have as much shine as you would like or is too shiny. To solve this, buy some clear acrylic varnish with a gloss, satin or matt finish, and apply a single coat of this on to the dry paint surface. Note that clear acrylic glaze looks like milk when wet but dries clear.

THE PAINT IS WAXY

If oil-based paint is not drying and has a waxy feel, this is a tricky problem to cure but careful preparation can often prevent it occurring. If you are painting on to a wooden surface you must first prime the surface. Primers provide not only a smooth surface on which to paint, but also a base on which the top colour will adhere well and dry and cure fully. If you have overlooked priming the surface, wash the troubled paint away with plenty of mineral turpentine and steel wool and start again.

If the paint is drying very slowly with a waxy feel to it then you have probably applied the coats too thickly. The surface of the paint is beginning to dry and cure and is sealing in the moisture underneath it. If you can, leave the paint for a week and see if it dries. If it does not dry, you will have to scrape it off, wash the wood with mineral turpentine and steel wool and start again. It is always better to paint more thin coats of paint than fewer thicker ones.

THE PRIMER IS NOT DRYING

This is a rare problem and is usually caused by the primer having been applied too thickly. Primer should be thin and soak into the new wood when applied, providing a smooth and even surface on which to apply the top colour. If the room in which you are working is damp you may also encounter problems with drying. Heating such a room will speed up the drying.

NOT ENOUGH PAINT

If you notice this potential disaster as the paint is running out, you can stretch your paint by diluting it with the appropriate thinner and by making sure that you use every drop of the paint that you have soaked your rollers and brushes with rather than washing it away into the sink. Sometimes you can buy a small tester pot of water-based colour to help with that last square metre. If you are working with a colour that you mixed for yourself, use the new mix on one complete wall or area so any slight variation will not be noticeable.

PAINT HAS BEEN SPILT

Spilling paint on the carpet is every painter's nightmare! If the paint spill is small, leave it to dry without touching it at all. It can then be removed from the carpet pile with abrasive sandpaper.

Water-based paint spills can be removed immediately by washing the area with plenty of water and blotting with clean rags. Larger oil-based spills will have to be washed with mineral turpentine and then with soapy water. Before beginning to wash a big spill, remove all the paint you possibly can by scraping up the paint from the outside of the spill to the centre. This prevents paint being spread any further.

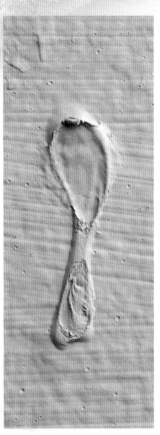

SAGGING

Paint has been applied too thickly or each coat has not been allowed to dry fully before the next was applied. To deal with sagging paint you must first allow it to dry fully and then rub the offending areas down with finishing paper or wet-and-dry sandpaper (use it wet for best results) until it is perfectly smooth. Then repaint.

CISSING

This term is used to describe the appearance of paint that is resisting the surface on to which it is being applied and usually occurs when water-based paint, such as acrylic paint, is being applied on to oil-based paint. For smaller areas, try washing the surface with detergent and a light scouring pad to remove any grease that may be sitting on the surface or give the surface a fine sand. If the paint still resists, you will have to resort to using oil-based paint. Proprietary brand deglossing agents are also available.

CRACKING

Cracking is caused when paint or acrylic clear varnish is applied over a base layer of paint or varnish of different elasticity before it has been given long enough to cure (which can take up to a month). For example, two separate brands of varnish may react with each other and form cracks. To deal with cracking you must allow the surface to dry fully and then rub it down with sandpaper ready for repainting. It may have to be sealed first. You could, however, consider leaving the cracking visible. It is a very popular ageing technique and can look very attractive in the right place.

DRIPS

Drips or 'nibs' in the dried paint surface should be left until the paint is dry. Rub the dried drip away with fine sandpaper and re-paint the area. On high-gloss finishes you may need to apply a final coat over the entire area to disguise the patch you rubbed away.

Product	Quality	Thinners and brush cleaning	Use for	Apply with
Wood primer	Preparation for bare wood. Prevents wood from swelling	Mineral turpentine or water (check the can)	Various porous surfaces such as bare wood	Brush
Undercoat	Matt finish, thin surface preparation and sealer	Water or mineral turpentine (check the can)	Various surfaces where required such as woodwork	Brush or roller
Matt	No shine, general-purpose coverage	Water	Walls, ceilings, primed or bare wood furniture. Often used on kitchen projects	Large brush or roller
Low sheen	Dull satin sheen, general-purpose coverage	Water	Walls, base for acrylic glaze work	Large brush or roller
Oil-based satin or semi gloss	Satin sheen, general-purpose coverage	Mineral turpentine	Walls, woodwork. Base coat for oil-based scumble glaze	Large brush or roller
Oil-based scumble glaze	Transparent	Mineral turpentine	Mix with artist's oil colours to make coloured glaze. Dragging and ragging	Brush or roller
Acrylic scumble glaze	Transparent	Water	Mix with artist's acrylic paints or colourizers	Brush or roller
Gloss	High shine, durable	Mineral turpentine or water (check the can)	Woodwork, doors	Good-quality brush
Woodstain	Thin colour without acrylic clear varnish for bare wood that soaks into wood grain	Water or mineral turpentine	Bare or unvarnished wood	Lint-free cloth or brush

Number of coats	Washable?	Area per litre (one coat) Square metres	Notes	Drying time before re-coating	Drying time final coat	Undercoat
I	N/A	I2	Rub down with sandpaper when dry	Oil based 16–24 hours Water based 4 hours	N/A	No
I	N/A	I2	Stir well. Rub down with sandpaper when dry	Oil based 8 hours Water based 2 hours	N/A	N/A
2	A little	I0	Used in this book for colour-washes. Mixed with acrylic scumble glaze	2–4 hours	8 hours	No but dilute first coat
2	Yes, soapy water. Do not scrub	I0	Some dark colours may require 3 or more coats	4 hours	8 hours	No
2	Yes, household cleaners. Avoid ammonia	I5	Traditionally oil based but now available with acrylic base	16–24 hours	24 hours	Primer or commercial undercoat
I	No	10–12 Depends on consistency	Good workability for ½ hour	6 hours	Leave 2 days before varnishing	Oil-based semi gloss
I	No	15–20	Work quickly to keep wet edge. Often used in this book with water-based paint	I hour	Overnight	Acrylic low sheen
2	Yes, household cleaners. Avoid ammonia	I2	Slow to apply—use good quality, bristle brush. Oil based is more hardwearing than acrylic	Oil based 16–24 hours Acrylic based 4–8 hours	24 hours	Primer/ undercoat
I or 2	No	8	Apply generously with brush or cloth. When dry, wipe away excess with a dry cloth. To protect the wood always wax or varnish when dry	Water based 2 hours Oil based 6–12 hours	Product varies	No

23

Product	Quality	Thinners and brush cleaning	Use for	Apply with
Varnish: polyurethane	Oil-based wood and paintwork protection. Choice of sheen	White spirit	Wood and to protect paintwork	Good-quality brush
Varnish: acrylic	Fast-drying protection for wood and paintwork. Choice of sheen. Non-yellowing	Water	Wood and to protect paintwork	Brush or roller
Wax	Protection and shine for wood	N/A	Bare or stained wood	Lint-free cloth
Craft paint	Intense colours for detailing and small areas	Various	Small craft projects	Soft brush
Artist's oil crayons and pastels	Intense, pure colours in stick form	Oil or turpentine	Detailing and drawing on walls, furniture or paper	N/A
Pigment	Intense colours	Water	Make homemade paints for colourwashing	Brush or roller
Glass paint	Semi transparent	Acetone/water	Painting tiles/bottles. Transparent detail work	Soft artist's brush
Acrylic-based satin	Satin sheen. General-purpose coverage	Walls	Walls, woodwork. Base coat for acrylic scumble glaze	Brush or roller
PVA glue	General-purpose sealer	Water	Walls in poor condition, 'thirsty' woodwork	Brush

Number of coats	Washable?	Area per litre (one coat) Square metres	Notes	Drying time before re-coating	Drying time final coat	Undercoat
Usually 2	Yes, soapy water	14	Use thinned and apply several coats for the greatest lustre. May yellow as coats build up	16-24 hours	24 hours	N/A
Usually 2	Yes	10	Difficult to apply as evenly as polyurethane varnishes. Not as durable but quick drying and crystal clear. Do not use on oil-based paints	1 hour	8 hours	No
1	Wipeable	8	Apply just like shoe polish, buff with a soft cloth between coats. Pure beeswax best for new wood	3 hours	N/A	Woodstain (optional)
1 or 2	Yes, do not scrub	N/A	Better quality than poster paints. Widely available in small quantities	½ hour	N/A	N/A
N/A	No	N/A	Allow to dry for 3 weeks or more before varnishing	N/A	N/A	N/A
1	Yes	Depends on medium used	Can be mixed with oil- or water-based products	Depends on medium used	Depends on medium used	Depends on medium used
1	Yes if type that is cured in oven	N/A	Brushstrokes always show up; beautiful vivid colour selection	1 hour	4 hours	No
2	Yes	12	Not as smooth or tough as oil-based satin. Excellent base for acrylic scumble glaze	4 hours	8 hours	Primer or undercoat
1	Yes, soapy water	12	Dilute 1:1 with water. Apply with brush	1–2 hours	N/A	N/A

Preparation

Preparation for all decoration is very important. Although it can be very time consuming, good preparation is worth every effort as it will improve the finished result no end.

REMOVING DUST

After sanding make sure you have a clean and dust-free environment. Dust down the doors with a dusting brush, making sure that no fine dust is left in the corners or mouldings. Then wipe over surfaces with a tack cloth. This is a small sticky cloth that can be wiped over a surface to remove any remaining dust. Unfold and refold the tack cloth, as necessary, for cleaner, stickier sections. Tack cloths are available at decorating shops in individually sealed packets. When you are not using the cloth, keep it in a sealed packet or it will dry out and lose its stickiness.

MASKING EDGES

Use masking tape to protect the worktop and any appliances in the kitchen from paint. Stick tape along the adjoining edge, but don't stick tape to the adjoining wall as this could pull off the paint with it. To paint edges of a wall, push a brush very carefully into the edge.

PROTECTING THE FLOOR

Even if you intend to be extremely neat and tidy in your decorating, always cover the floor well with dust or plastic sheets. Plastic sheets provide more protection as paint cannot leak through them, although they can be slippery to walk on. Cover the worktops with plastic at the same time for protection against spills.

PREPARING WALLS

All the walls in this book have been painted in matt water-based paint. Holes and cracks can be filled, sanded down and painted straight over in water-based paint. If you have newly plastered walls, allow a drying-out period of about six months as small hairline cracks will appear through the paint as the plaster dries out. Bare plaster should be sealed first. For colourwashed walls, a rollered surface is the best to work on. Remember that imperfections will show up more once a colourwash is applied as will areas that have not been covered sufficiently. A common miss are the edges and corners that are painted in with a brush. Make sure that these areas are covered well.

ADHESION

Kitchen units and doors get so much wear and tear that any paint finish must not only be well sealed for protection but most importantly the paint must stick well to the surface and not chip off. Paint adhesion must be considered at every stage of decorating. It is no use sealing a finish with a tough varnish if the original coat of paint has not stuck sufficiently to the base coat.

The projects in this book have used water-based acrylic paint together with artist's acrylic paints. These particular paints can never be applied to an oil-based finish as they will just not adhere. The surface must be porous and primer is an ideal porous surface to paint on. To apply primer to most surfaces, rub down the surface well with sandpaper to provide a key for the primer to adhere, then apply the water-based coat. Always check the instructions for each product you use; they vary considerably. Wood and medium density fibreboard (MDF) are the easiest surfaces to paint. Formica and laminated doors are the hardest. Many paint manufacturers do not advise painting such surfaces but it can be done if you rub the surface down well with sandpaper to provide a key before applying primer. Use tile primer on non-porous surfaces.

VARNISHING

Water-based paint is usually used on ceilings and walls, while satin and gloss enamel, which are much harder and tougher paints, are usually used on doors and woodwork. As water-based paint is not necessarily made for wear and tear, it may be protected with acrylic clear varnish. Remember to use the correct varnish for the type of paint you use. For the water-based finishes in this book, a tough acrylic dead flat varnish was used. Acrylic varnish is also available in satin and gloss finishes, but the dead flat matt seemed most appropriate for the finishes in this book. Acrylic varnish does not yellow in the way oil-based varnish will but it does deepen the colour, even in the dead flat matt form. At least two coats of varnish are required for a good finish.

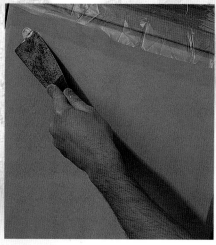
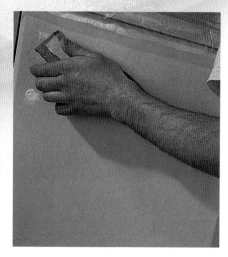

CLEANING SURFACES

Paint will not stick to a greasy and dirty surface so all surfaces should be cleaned prior to being painted. Sugar soap is a very powerful surface cleanser designed especially for use in the decorating trade. It is tough and cuts through grease, grime and nicotine. Wear rubber gloves at all times when using sugar soap, and protect work surfaces and floors from any possible spillage.

To use sugar soap, first check your individual product instructions, and add warm water to the sugar soap accordingly. Apply this mixture with a brush or a cloth to the surface to be cleaned and then rinse with clean water.

FILLING HOLES AND CRACKS

There are many different surface fillers available for different applications. Filler can either be bought in powder form to be mixed up with water, or as a ready-made creamy paste. Fine surface filler is ideal for intricate repairs, but an all-purpose filler should be used for deeper cavities. The filler will tend to sink into a hole so fill over and above the hole to enable this to be sanded down to a flat finish afterwards. If the hole is particularly deep, fill as much as you can first with small pieces or chips of wood, and then use filler for the remaining space.

Instant flexible filler is best for sealing sides and edges and areas prone to movement, for example where the kitchen door meets the wall. It is applied through a tube and wiped smooth with a damp cloth. It cannot be sanded down and should not be used for surface holes.

To apply filler, smear a small amount into the hole using a filling knife. As the filler tends to sink in as it dries, fill over and above the hole. Leave to dry.

SANDING

Sandpaper is available in many different grades, from very coarse to very fine. If the paper you have is too coarse, tear it in two and rub it together to grind it down for a smoother abrasion. If you are sanding a whole door, start with a coarser paper (if required) and work up to a finer grade to finish.

Wet-and-dry sandpaper is good for achieving a super fine glass-like finish on a surface. This is only really applicable for oil-based semi gloss finishes and especially gloss paint. This very fine paper is used wet and rubbed onto the surface. You can wrap the sandpaper around a sanding block to make rubbing down easier. The sanding block in the photograph was bought from a decorating shop, and is made from cork, but you could use any very flat material such as a smooth piece of wood.

Once the filler is completely dry, rub the surface down with sandpaper wrapped around a sanding block for a smooth and flawless finish. Wipe away any dust with a tack cloth.

MAKEOVER PROJECT

Tuscan Blue

This strong rich blue is taken from an old country kitchen in Provence or Tuscany. The colour is of cornflowers and deep blue glass. As the blue is slightly violet in tone, it has the effect of warming the room wonderfully, while the pale walls prevent the effect from becoming overpowering.

The blue paint has been chipped and cracked, showing patches of a brownish-grey base to give the effect of age. For a stronger antiqued effect you could use a lighter base colour. Alternatively, you could use strong colours together such as

PROJECTS FROM THIS
MAKEOVER SHOW YOU

• HOW TO CREATE A
  CHIPPED PAINT EFFECT

• HOW TO ANTIQUE WITH
  CRACKLE GLAZE

• HOW TO DECORATE A
  CHAIR

• HOW TO COVER BOXES
  WITH FABRIC

turquoise and deep blue, or bright green and deep blue. Experiment first with little tester pots of paint—you might be surprised at the colours you end up choosing!

The walls in this kitchen were painted in an off-white colour, then washed with an older dirtier white. In this way, the central areas are kept lighter while the corners, edges and sides are darkened, giving a softer antiqued look rather than an even colourwash. It also softens the newness of a flat painted wall.

The table and chairs were painted in the darker wall colour and the chairs were given a simple handpainted flower motif in the same blue as used on the cupboard doors. Leftover paint can be used on all sorts of things!

The door knobs on the units are small wooden knobs which have been given the same paint effect as the doors. Try to buy untreated wooden knobs to paint as they will not need to be prepared.

This cracked antiqued look is particularly good for cupboards needing repair, as any lumps and bumps in the doors just add to the effect—as will any further knocks and chips. This look also disguises any repairs you make with filler; you won't have to worry about sanding to create smooth surfaces. However, remember that once you use crackle glaze on your doors it is very difficult to paint over.

CREATING A CHIPPED PAINT EFFECT

This decorating technique is very effective in achieving a mellow look of age and wear through time, an effect that has become very popular and an interesting way to break up solid colour. The chipped paint effect can be used in conjunction with crackle glaze (see page 32), as can be seen in this Tuscan blue kitchen.

1 Apply a base coat on the surface and leave to dry. Using a thin paintbrush, carefully apply small lumps of beeswax to the surface. The areas to concentrate on most are the edges and corners as these are the most likely places to receive the brunt of any wear and tear.

2 Allow the beeswax to dry overnight and then apply the water-based top coat. If you will not be using crackle glaze (see page 32), two coats of water-based paint will be required.

3 Allow the paint to dry, then carefully chip off the lumps of beeswax using a filling knife. This will reveal small patches of the base coat, giving the effect of age. Apply a coat of acrylic clear varnish over the surface to seal it.

EXPERT TIPS

• *A chipped paint effect can also be used in conjunction with colour-ageing (see page 58) to enhance further the antiqued look of a piece.*

• *For a flatter, softer worn effect, rub a candle or a wax stick along the surface, concentrating on the door edges. Unlike the beeswax the candle can be painted over immediately—the paint will not stick to the waxed area and can be rubbed off quite easily.*

Antiquing with crackle glaze

Using crackle glaze on a surface has the effect of making the paintwork crack, giving it a worn and aged look. The effect can be used on its own or together with the chipped paint effect, as seen on the blue kitchen units. To use both together, apply the crackle glaze straight onto the beeswax before applying the paint. This project illustrates how to use crackle glaze on its own.

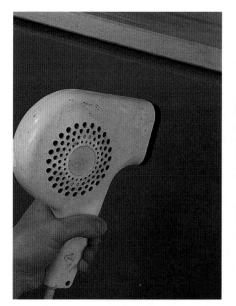

1 Using a household paintbrush, apply crackle glaze over the surface in an up-and-down motion. Keep all of the brushstrokes even and regular as this will help determine the direction of the cracks. Allow to dry.

2 Once the crackle glaze is dry, apply a coat of dark blue matt water-based paint, keeping the brushstrokes even and straight in an up-and-down direction. Don't stop the brushstroke halfway down the surface as this could show up later in the cracks.

3 Leave the paint to dry and wait for the cracks to appear. To speed up the drying time, you can dry the paint gently with a hairdryer, moving the hairdryer all over the surface.

4 When the cracks appear, dab a clean cotton cloth into diluted pale blue water-based paint and rub this into the surface; this will highlight the cracks and break up the colour. When dry, apply two coats of acrylic matt varnish to seal.

EXPERT TIPS

• *Experiment to see how the cracks will appear by testing a small area first. You could apply either one or two coats of crackle glaze (two for larger cracks), but always follow the instructions for your individual product as they do vary from one product to another.*

• *Once you have used crackle glaze on a surface it is difficult to re-paint it as the glaze will keep on working and cracks will keep on appearing. To overcome this, sand down the surface to remove the crackle glaze. Alternatively, cover the surface with a fine surface filler, then seal this with shellac to prevent the glaze coming through any more. This is a laborious process and best avoided!*

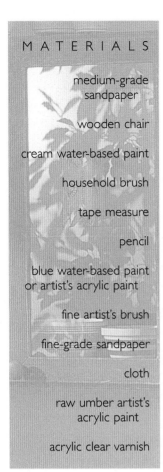

MATERIALS

medium-grade
sandpaper

wooden chair

cream water-based paint

household brush

tape measure

pencil

blue water-based paint
or artist's acrylic paint

fine artist's brush

fine-grade sandpaper

cloth

raw umber artist's
acrylic paint

acrylic clear varnish

Decorating a chair

Painting old furniture is a good way to disguise unsightly cracks and holes; these can simply be repaired and filled and then covered with paint, never to be seen again. Before painting a chair with water-based paint, you need to rub it down to remove any varnish, wax or previous paint layers, plus any dirt and grease, then apply a coat of primer. Alternatively, you could use an oil-based paint, such as satin enamel; in this case, you then need to use oil-based paint for the painted pattern. It is important not to mix oil and acrylic materials. This chair was painted with water-based paint on top of a coat of white primer. The design—a simple pattern of dots—was applied by hand, varnished, and finally coloured and aged with a small amount of artist's acrylic raw umber.

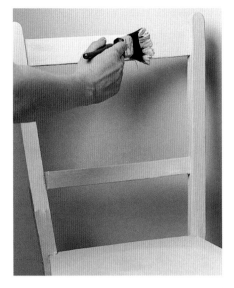

• Turn the chair upside down first and paint the underside before finishing off with the chair the right way up.

• Apply any number of colours and patterns in this technique to suit your environment.

• More intricate patterns could be applied by stencil, which would achieve a more even and regular pattern. It is more time consuming to cut a stencil, but for a set of chairs, where the same stencil could be used, it would in fact be quicker.

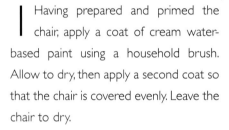

1 Having prepared and primed the chair, apply a coat of cream water-based paint using a household brush. Allow to dry, then apply a second coat so that the chair is covered evenly. Leave the chair to dry.

2 Measure the backrest of the chair, then mark out regular positions for the dotted pattern with a pencil. The blue to be used for the pattern is dark enough to cover the pencil mark but if using lighter colours it is best to use a paler marker such as chalk.

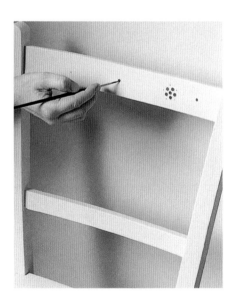

3 Mix up a small amount of blue paint for the design, using either water-based or artist's acrylic paint. Using a fine artist's brush, carefully paint in the floral dots, following the pencil marks. Leave to dry, then rub the painted pattern lightly with fine-grade sandpaper.

4 Use a tack cloth to wipe away any dust left by the sandpaper. Mix a little raw umber artist's acrylic paint with acrylic clear varnish, then brush this over the chair to create an aged look. If the brown looks too heavy, wipe it off quick-ly before it dries, and try again.

Covering boxes with fabric

Boxes can be covered with fabric in any number of ways, according to the shape and style desired. The three boxes shown here are old biscuit tins—one square, one round and one hexagonal. They were covered with thin checked fabric, but you could use thicker upholstery fabric if preferred. The fabric was stuck down with glue and trimmed with a thick ribbon to create a neat and tidy edge. The ribbon used here is plain, but there is a wonderful array of trimmings available from haberdashery stores for you to choose from.

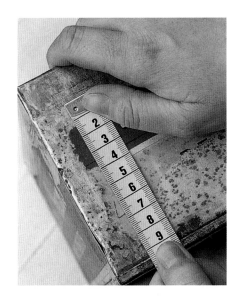

1 Measure the tin and cut the fabric accordingly. As thin fabric was to be used here, it was first doubled and ironed flat. (If using thicker fabric, you do not need to double it.) If the lid of the tin is tight fitting, make sure that you stop the fabric under the section that rubs against the lid.

2 Apply fabric glue to the box, along one side at a time, then stick down the fabric neatly and smoothly on top. Follow the manufacturer's advice concerning application and drying times as these can vary.

3 Fold over or trim the corners to cover a square lid. This cover has been folded crisply for a neat finish. If you prefer to trim the corners, cut a square shape from each corner, then fold the edges down neatly.

4 For optional extra decoration, a piece of smaller checked fabric in the same colours as the larger checks can be laid over the tin in a strip. Turn the edges under and iron the strip to achieve neat side edges. Then apply glue over the fabric-covered tin, and carefully stick the fabric down on top.

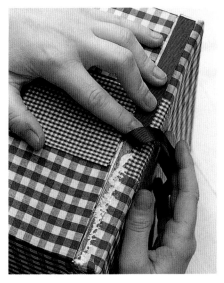

5 Choose a ribbon trim to suit your particular box and fabric. Apply glue to the sides of the box, or the ribbon trim itself, then stick it down firmly in position. Allow the glue to dry.

EXPERT TIPS

• Thin fabric is fine for tins that are not handled too often. However, it is easier to brush tougher upholstery fabric clean. For tins that are used more frequently, plastic fabric is preferable.

• Some biscuit tins, such as the round and hexagonal ones shown here, have a thin metal edging. This can either be painted with enamel paint or left as it is, as thin trimming fits neatly inside it.

MAKEOVER PROJECT

Neutral Shades

Pale creamy colours are the most popular for painted kitchens. These subtle natural shades form a gentle, relaxing and undemanding background that will enable you to bring colour into the room in other ways.

Look at natural objects for inspiration when choosing soft neutral colours for your kitchen scheme. Pebbles and seashells can be found in beautiful subtle shades in every colour. Look closely at such everyday food as garlic cloves, rice, bread and cheese for pale neutral shades.

PROJECTS FROM THIS
MAKEOVER SHOW YOU

- HOW TO BLEND AND
  MIX COLOURS

- HOW TO PAINT A
  WALL PATTERN

- HOW TO STAIN A FLOOR

- HOW TO PAINT AND
  DECORATE TINS

The crackled tiles in the kitchen were the starting point for this colour scheme. The tiles contained pink and grey tones with dark grey cracks. The pink was echoed on the walls with a very light colourwash. To do this, a pale pink was washed on to the walls first and then softened with a semi transparent white wash and very small amounts of grey here and there. This was warmed up in places with touches of gardenia (the colour of clotted cream). For colourwashing in gentle colours, it is best to buy shades that are darker than you actually require and then lighten them with white paint. Once the paint is diluted and added to scumble glaze it appears much lighter, so if you use subtle shades to begin with they are likely to be lost in the finished effect.

The painted wall pattern was used to echo the shape and colours of the tiles along the wall. This pattern was made up on the spot but you could design your own pattern in any number of ways. You could, for example, make a border of straight lines or turn the squares on their edge to make a pattern of diamonds.

Gardenia was also used as the base colour for the unit doors. It helped to bring together the cream tones in the beech worktop and the pale pine wood floor. Soft grey was applied over the creamy, gardenia base in downward streaks; this was then followed by white (see below). The door knobs were painted in the same way; the darker grey tones remaining in the recesses accentuate their shape. This same process could also be used for panelled doors.

BLENDING COLOURS

This method of blending colours on a surface is easy to do, but it is best to experiment first on a piece of cardboard or lining paper until you achieve an effect you are happy with.

1 Spoon some grey water-based paint and some acrylic scumble glaze into a paint tray without mixing them together. Dip a household paintbrush first into the paint and then the glaze, and then paint this in downward strokes on to the surface to be decorated. Keep the colour light and even.

2 Allow the paint and glaze coat to dry. Then dip your brush lightly into white water-based paint so that only a tiny amount of paint is on the bristles, and brush this roughly over the top, allowing streaks of the grey to show through. Continue to paint over the surface until the colours are blended to your liking.

EXPERT TIPS

• For a softer blended effect, dip the brush into more scumble glaze—this will keep the paint wetter and more workable.

• This method of blending colours is a very subtle effect and is best achieved with two very similar shades of colour. Do not use colours that will not blend into each other naturally. It is always helpful to see how such colours blend in nature, such as pebbles or shells.

Painting a wall pattern

This simple wall pattern is painted using water-based paint onto a water-based colourwash. A colourwashed wall gives a gentle background for such handpainted patterns or stencils. To create this shape you can draw around a wall tile. To paint more intricate shapes and patterns, you may find it easier to cut a stencil or use transfer paper to transfer a design (see page 65).

MATERIALS

ruler

pencil

wall tile

flat fitch or artist's brush

water-based paint

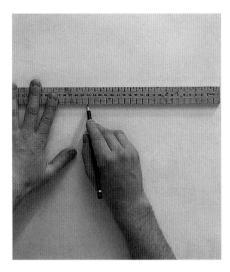

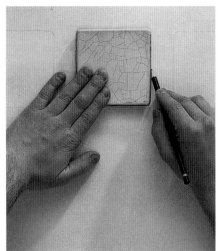

1 Measure the wall and decide where you would like the pattern shapes to go. Mark the positions lightly on the wall with a pencil. These marks will be used as positional guides when drawing the design on the wall.

2 Following the positional guides, draw lightly around the wall tile with a pencil to build up the wall pattern. This can extend over a whole wall or just a small area. A random pattern can look effective, but if you prefer you can make a strong geometric design with precise angles. Do not worry about the pencil marks; they will be covered with paint at the next stage.

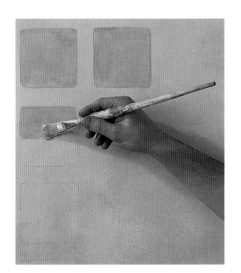

3 Using a flat fitch or artist's brush, paint in the pencilled shapes with water-based paint, without going over the edges. For an even softer effect, you could go over this pattern with a light colourwash. You will have to colourwash the whole wall for an even shade.

EXPERT TIPS
• *To make the pattern appear less solid, add some acrylic scumble glaze to the water-based paint. Put a small amount of scumble glaze and a separate small amount of water-based paint in the paint tray and dip into both with your brush. Use the paint tray like a palette and test the consistency first. Build the colour up slowly. It is always easier to make the colour stronger—but more difficult to remove the paint to achieve a lighter shade. If you find the squares too dark, you will have to paint them white and start again.*

• *For an even softer effect, you could go over this pattern with a light colourwash. You will have to colourwash the whole wall for an even shading.*

MATERIALS

floorboards

protective face mask

floor sander

edger

knotting solution

cloth or brush

artist's acrylic paints

water

bucket

household brush

cloth

acrylic flat or satin floor
varnish

Staining a floor

This project shows how to create a natural-looking stained effect on pine floorboards. Many proprietary woodstains can look rather heavy and unnatural, and yet untouched pine can look rather flat and new—not as mellow as the effect achieved here. The way to create this effect is an unconventional treatment but one that works easily, and, once varnished, is as durable as any other floor finish.

A wash of thinned artist's acrylic paint is applied to the wood and gently rubbed with a cloth to achieve a shading that looks natural and mellow. Two or three artist's acrylic paints can be mixed to achieve the precise colour required. The resulting colours are generally of good quality, usually a purer more intense colour than that achieved with a water-based colourwash.

1 Check your floorboards for loose nails. Then, wearing a protective face mask, sand the floorboards with a floor sander. Floor sanders can be hired; always follow given instructions. Most sanders have a dust bag but still produce a large quantity of fine dust. Start by using coarse-grade sandpaper, if necessary, and gradually work your way down to fine-grade sandpaper.

2 Use an edger to reach right into the corners and edges of the floor. These can be hired with floor sanders. As with a floor sander, always work from a coarse-grade to a fine-grade sandpaper to produce a smooth finish.

3 Seal any knots in new wood to prevent them from bleeding resin. Apply knotting solution over any knots using a cloth or brush. For pale wood floorboards, such as pine, use white knotting solution, which dries transparent. Apply the solution only to the knot. As the solution seals the knot and wood, the stain will not soak in as effectively as it will on untreated areas.

4 Squirt a small amount of artist's acrylic paints from their tubes into a bucket and slowly dilute them by adding water a little at a time. Stir the mix constantly. Test the stain first on a piece of wood. Apply the wash over the floorboards in sweeping brushstrokes in the direction of the grain. Rub off areas that may appear too heavy with a cloth.

5 Allow the stain to dry completely, then apply two or three coats of acrylic flat or satin floor varnish over the surface. Do not use oil-based varnish as this will yellow and ruin the subtlety of the staining effect.

EXPERT TIPS

• *Before staining floorboards, make sure that the floor is dust free. Wipe the floor with a tack cloth to remove tiny specks of dust.*

• *If the grain of the wood rises when you apply a water stain, allow it to dry thoroughly then lightly sand it off to a smoother finish.*

MATERIALS

tin

masking tape or paper tape

cream enamel spray paint

lining brush

green enamel paint

cloth

mineral turpentine

Painting tins

With the extensive range of enamel spray paints now available, it has never been easier and quicker to paint onto metal. Spray paints are ideal for quick and even coverage, and for stencilling, while the variety of colours available in small tins is useful for painting details. Old biscuit tins can be transformed to suit the colours of your kitchen. The tins here feature a simple lining design in dark green—but you can paint any kind of motif or pattern. Enamel paints provide a hardwearing finish and do not require varnish of any kind.

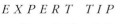

1 | Mask off the inside of the tin so that no paint is sprayed inside. This wide paper tape is useful as only one edge is sticky; cover the surrounding area well with newspaper or protective plastic when spraying paint. This paint is not easy to remove from areas it should not reach!

2 | Following the instructions on the spray can, shake the can for at least a minute, then spray cream enamel paint over the tin as evenly as possible, holding the can about 20–30 cm (8–12 in) away from the tin. It is best to apply several thin coats of paint rather than one thick one. If the paint is applied too heavily it will run and produce drips.

EXPERT TIP

• If you find it difficult to achieve a steady line while painting free-hand, use low-tack masking tape as a guide. However, do check first that this tape will not pull off the base coat of paint. Stick strips of low-tack tape first to your clothing to reduce the tackiness before attaching it to the tin.

3 | Allow the cream paint to dry for at least 24 hours, then paint lining details around the rim using a small lining brush and green enamel paint. Hold the tin so that your finger slides along the edge, acting as a guide. If you do make a mistake, wipe it off immediately with a cloth dipped in mineral turpentine.

4 | Paint lines on the tin lid to complete the decoration. Always follow the natural curves and mouldings of the tin to keep a neat edging. Allow the paint to dry thoroughly before using the tin.

MAKEOVER PROJECT

Moroccan Spice

The colours featured in this warm, mellow kitchen —rich, earthy terracottas and vivid blue-greens— evoke the colours of Morocco, and the warm spicy tones of chilli powder, nutmeg and turmeric.

Exotic Morocco was the inspiration for this kitchen. Naturally colourwashed walls, earthy terracotta-coloured pots, exotic tiles and ceramics and vivid blue-green patterning all work together to create a warm and lively atmosphere.

The cupboard doors are warm orangey browns with some greyer tones in the patterning. These

PROJECTS FROM THIS
MAKEOVER SHOW YOU

- HOW TO PAINT A DOOR

- HOW TO TRANSFER A
  PATTERN

- HOW TO MAKE A MOSAIC
  TABLETOP

- HOW TO STRIP AN OLD
  WOODEN CHAIR

- HOW TO ANTIQUE
  A TABLE

greyer, more muddy, colours were taken from the colours in the floor. The deep chilli red was added to the door pattern and to a simple pattern of dots along the edge of the shelf. Although these warm colours seem to advance towards you and therefore have the effect of making the room look smaller, they also seem to increase the temperature of the room, making for a warm and cosy kitchen.

The units were painted with a sand-coloured base and then washed in a light spicy red, which produced a slightly mottled base colour. A Moroccan pattern was then painted over this using transfer paper. This particular pattern was adapted from a Moroccan tile design of which there are hundreds to be found in design source books; you could also look through travel books and holiday photographs or kitchen accessories for design ideas and inspiration.

The walls were washed a few times in light sandy colours on a base of white water-based paint. The wash was built up with three layers of colour, one slightly yellow, one more muddy and the other more orangey brown. The window frames and surround were painted in a muddier colour found in the painted pattern on the doors. The dark wooden floor and the wooden worktop fitted in well with these earthy tones.

PAINTING A DOOR

This basic technique is very simple but one that many people do not know. Applying paint correctly gives you a good, even coverage of paint and it may mean only having to apply one coat instead of two. The mistake a lot of people make is trying to apply paint in an up-and-down motion—it is much more difficult to achieve an even application in this way. To paint an average-sized kitchen door, a 6.5 cm (2½ in) household brush is particularly suitable.

EXPERT TIP
• *If you have panelled doors, a different method of painting applies. First paint the centre frame beading and the panels. Then paint the outer edge—the two horizontal top and bottom bars first, then the two vertical sides. Apply paint vertically for the panels and the vertical sides (stiles) and then horizontally for the cross bars (rails).*

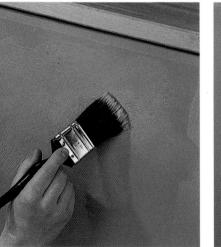

1 Starting in the centre of a door and working quickly, apply the paint liberally in every direction, up, down, side to side and diagonally, to cover the whole surface completely.

2 Then, without pausing, brush the wet paint down, up and down again over the entire surface to smooth and even out the application. Work at speed so that the paint remains moveable; if you leave the paint to dry slightly before smoothing the brushstrokes, the result will look uneven and streaky.

tape measure

plain or graph paper

pencil

low-tack masking tape

transfer paper

fine artist's brush

acrylic paint

Transferring a pattern

This method is a simple way of transferring a pattern, and for an intricate pattern such as this one, it is easier to use this transfer method than to cut and use a stencil. Transfer paper can be bought in different colours—blue is the most common, but on a darker base yellow or white would stand out better. The transfer paper is water based so once the pattern has been painted on, any remaining marks can be wiped off very easily with a damp cloth.

First draw the pattern onto graph paper—you can always use a photocopier to enlarge and reduce your design to fit particular doors.

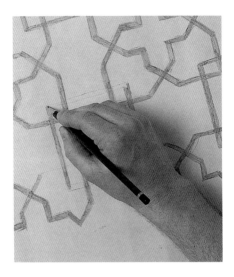

1 Measure the cupboard doors with a tape measure. Then cut a piece of paper the same size as the doors and draw out your pattern on the paper in pencil. You could copy a pattern from a tile design like this one, from a design source book, or you could even design your own pattern.

2 Using low-tack tape, stick a sheet of transfer paper on to the cupboard, chalky side down. Then tape the pencilled design on top of this. Using a pencil, trace over the design outlines to transfer the pattern onto the door. When you have finished, lift up one corner of the transfer paper to check that all of the design has transferred. If necessary, go over any faint lines again. Then remove the paper.

3 Using a fine artist's brush and acrylic paint, carefully paint over the transferred lines. You could vary the colour throughout the pattern just by dipping the brush occasionally into another very similar colour. Don't worry if your painted line wobbles slightly as you paint—this adds to the handpainted charm of your design.

EXPERT TIPS

• *Draw the different elements of a design on tracing paper before transferring them on to the main sheet. In this way, an even scale can be retained. Mark the actual door size onto the page and draw the design to fit as neatly as possible.*

• *An alternative method is to use photocopies of your design. These could be enlarged and reduced to scale, then stuck together with sticky tape.*

• *It is also helpful to draw a rough colour sketch before you start, as certain patterns work best with certain colour combinations.*

• *Once the pattern is complete and if you feel it looks a little strong, lightly rub it back with fine-grade sandpaper or add a coloured varnish (like that used in the painted chair project, page 34).*

Making a mosaic table

MATERIALS

table

glass tiles

tile nippers

protective eye goggles

tape measure

pencil, optional

PVA glue

ready-mixed grout

flexible spatula

cloth

This simple mosaic design was created using small glass tiles—the kind often used at the bottom of swimming pools. The tiles can be bought loose, but are usually supplied on a paper backing, which is easily removed after being soaked in water. The tiles in this design were cut and applied to a wooden tabletop that had been scratched and damaged beyond repair. Mosaic tiles can be applied to most surfaces—even an old plastic tabletop can be transformed with mosaic tiles. They provide a hardwearing surface that is also practical for garden furniture outdoors. The tiles are available in a vast range of colours and the design can be as complicated as you like. This table features a simple circular design but you could create a more detailed pattern and cut the tiles to fit.

1 Cut a few tiles with tile nippers to experiment with different pattern formations. Wear protective eye goggles when using tile nippers to protect against flying fragments of tile. Angle the nippers over one half of the tile rather than all the way across when cutting it. This will achieve a more precise cut and prevent the tile from shattering.

2 Arrange the tiles in the desired pattern, experimenting with whole and cut shapes to see what works best. This design uses both whole tiles around the edge and cut tiles in the centre. Measure the tabletop and ensure that the design will fit. For a complicated design, you can draw the design out on the tabletop and cut the tiles to fit.

3 Using a strong PVA glue or panel adhesive, stick the tiles down in place on the tabletop, leaving small gaps in between. Tile adhesive can be used for quicker applications, but sticking tiles individually allows you to work more slowly. Run your fingers over the glued tiles to ensure they are secure.

4 Apply ready-mixed grout over the glued tiles using a flexible spatula. Cover the entire surface, then wipe off excess grout with a damp cloth. Grout will remain in the spaces between the tiles. Allow the grout to dry, then clean the tiles with a damp cloth.

EXPERT TIPS
- *To create a more subtle effect, use small ceramic tiles in place of glass tiles. These are supplied in uneven shapes and have a rich natural colouring to them. They are more expensive than the glass tiles but for small areas and intricate patterns the effect can be stunning.*

- *Another, cheaper alternative would be to use broken crockery. Break old plates and saucers gently with a hammer to produce random shapes that can be used to build up a colourful and interesting mosaic pattern.*

Stripping an old wooden chair

It is always risky to strip painted chairs as you never know what you might find underneath. The worst scenario would be to find splits and cracks and holes stuffed with filler, but there is always the chance that you might uncover beautiful wood that can be cleaned and restored to its original beauty. Stripping is a messy job and best done outside in the fresh air so you do not inhale any noxious fumes, but it is well worth the effort when you discover a beautiful grain.

There are several different ways of stripping wood. This project illustrates two approaches, one using proprietary paint and varnish stripper and the other using an electric heat gun. Both of these methods will remove layers of heavy gloss paint.

1a Using a heat gun, burn off the old layers of paint, scraping off the burnt paint with a paint scraper as you go along. This shape of scraper is useful for getting into corners. Once the paint has been burned off, proceed to step 4.

1b Alternatively, apply paint stripper with a brush, dabbing it liberally onto the chair. Work in a well-ventilated area, preferably outside, as the fumes can be toxic and harmful. Always wear protective gloves when working with paint stripper.

2 Leave the stripper for about 15 minutes to work into the paint (check the manufacturer's instructions), then scrape off the paint with a scraper. Collect the scrapings and throw them away. This whole process may need to be repeated if some paint still remains.

3 Still wearing protective gloves, dip a pad of steel wool in mineral turps and rub this over the entire chair, including all tight corners and edges, to remove any remaining paint stripper and clean right into the wood grain. Leave to dry.

4 After being stripped, wood tends to be rather dry, and benefits from a nourishing layer of wax. Once dry and clean, apply furniture wax over the wood with a pad of fine steel wool. Allow to dry according to the manufacturer's instructions (usually about 20 minutes), then buff to a sheen with a soft cloth.

EXPERT TIPS
• *By applying mineral turpentine to the chair (step 3), the grain will not tend to swell and lift which often happens when water is used on bare wood.*

• *To dispose of paint and varnish stripper safely, put it in a jam jar and take it to the local waste disposal site. Do not pour it down the sink or into a drain as it is highly toxic.*

Antiquing a table

This table was bought from a junk yard and was split and damaged—even some corners were missing. However, it was given a new lease of life with a distressed finish in a vibrant colour of turquoise. The damaged surface and missing corners took on a different sort of charm once the table was painted! This antiquing technique simply uses a few tester pots of water-based paint and works best on bare or primed wood; it will not work on surfaces that have been varnished or sealed as the water-based paint will not adhere properly. In this case, surfaces should be rubbed down well with sandpaper to provide a good key before a primer can be applied.

1 Fill in any large splits or holes in the table with wood filler, then rub the table down with sandpaper and wipe away the dust. Paint the table with a coat of primer so that it will accept water-based paint, then, when dry, apply a base coat of dark brown water-based paint. Allow this to dry out thoroughly.

2 Apply a coat of turquoise water-based paint over the dark brown base coat. Cover the surface completely, making sure that the paint reaches into every corner and inside edge of the table. Turn the table upside down as you work. Do not let this coat of paint dry out completely before the next step.

3 While the paint is still slightly wet, wipe off small patches from the edges and corners of the table with a cloth. These are the areas that would be the first to wear away naturally. Use a damp cloth or one dipped in methylated spirits on those areas that are drying too quickly. If the paint comes off too easily and smoothly, reapply it and start again.

4 Once the table is completely dry, seal it with two coats of dead flat matt clear acrylic varnish. This varnish dries quickly and can easily be recoated the same day. Depending on the temperature, it is usually recoatable after an hour.

EXPERT TIPS

• *If you find it difficult to judge the drying time for rubbing off the water-based paint, an alternative method is to apply wax to the edges of the table after the brown base coat is dry. Then paint over this with turquoise paint and later chip it off to reveal patches of the brown underneath. (See page 31 for instructions on this effect.)*

• *To distress a finish further, you can apply crackle glaze between the base and top coats (see terracotta pots on page 86).*

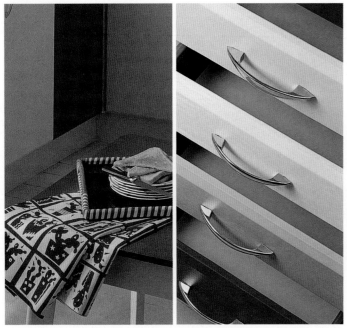

M A K E O V E R P R O J E C T

1950s Style

Simple and fun to paint, this colourful kitchen pays tribute to the design styles of the 1950s with its bright decoration, abstract designs and 1950s memorabilia. The resulting effect is a bright and lively kitchen which will cheer up your kitchen chores no end.

The 1950s design memorabilia is becoming ever more popular. More and more people are starting to cherish objects and furniture made in the fifties, which a few years ago they might have thrown away. The particular colours and designs are being

PROJECTS FROM THIS MAKEOVER SHOW YOU

• HOW TO PAINT TILES

• HOW TO COPY DESIGNS FROM FABRIC

• HOW TO MAKE CURTAINS FROM REMNANTS

• HOW TO CHANGE HANDLES ON UNITS

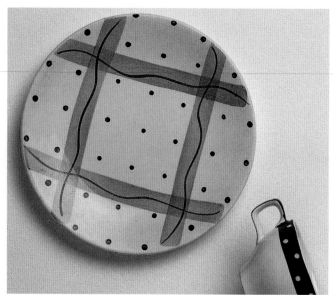

enjoyed and appreciated again in a completely different light.

The main inspiration for this kitchen was a pair of authentic 1950s curtains. This fabric featured a combination of mustard yellow with strong bright red, pale grey, pale greeny yellow and light cream and is typical of the time. You could base your 1950s colour scheme on any number of things—1950s crockery, a design from a bookcover, or even a biscuit tin.

The cupboard doors were painted separately in different strong colours. To counteract these vivid colours and echo the background of the fabric, the walls were painted in a soft almond white, while the floor and skirting board were painted in a more practical soft pale grey. As the floor consisted of untreated floorboards, it meant they could be painted in water-based paint, then sealed with tough water-based floor varnish. Alternatively, you could use satin paint or a proprietary floor paint instead.

The cupboard handles played a major part in achieving the 1950s look. The handles used here were stainless steel but you can always paint handles to match your own particular colour scheme. With any leftover paint you could paint other items in a similar style. In this kitchen some wooden chairs and the wall shelf were decorated, as was the little table shown in the centre of the room; this was found in a junk shop, cleaned up and painted to match the kitchen doors. A contrasting colour was used on the rim of the tabletop, a typical 1950s feature.

PAINTING TILES

Glazed tiles are non-absorbent surfaces which offer little, if any, adhesion for paints. However, they can be successfully painted provided the right preparation and paints are used. Never sand tiles, as this will scratch the surface, causing irreparable damage.

1 Wash the tiles with strong sugar soap or detergent, then rinse and allow to dry. Apply a thin coat of white oil-based satin paint to both the tiles and the grout. Leave to dry for at least 12 hours.

2 Using a small, flat brush, paint the surface of each tile in oil- or water-based gloss paint, making sure you do not paint over the grout. Apply two coats of paint, if necessary, allowing 24 hours drying time between each.

3 Once you have finished your colour design, allow the paint to dry. The entire surface may then be coated with an oil- or water-based clear varnish, but this is not absolutely necessary.

EXPERT TIPS
- *To protect tiles painted with water-based paints, seal them with clear acrylic floor varnish. This is very tough and will take all the wear and tear a splashback will require.*

- *Tiles painted with satin enamel paint will not need to be varnished. If you prefer to varnish them for durability, use an oil-based polyurethane floor varnish. However, this discolours the paint and is noticeable over pale colours.*

MATERIALS

plain paper

fabric

low-tack tape

transfer paper

pencil

fine artist's brush

artist's acrylic paints or
matt water-based paint

acrylic clear varnish

Copying elements from a fabric design

If your curtains form a strong element of your kitchen decor, copying elements from their design is a useful way of extending the theme onto other surfaces. By doing this, your whole decorating scheme is linked together with colour and pattern. Here, elements from the curtain fabric are copied on to the wall tiles.

1 Photocopy sections of the fabric you would like to use. This may be curtain fabric, as in this kitchen, tea towels or a tablecloth. Enlarge or reduce the design elements to the size you require.

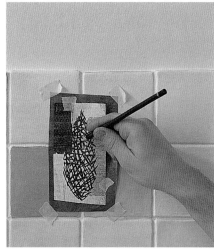

2 Using low-tack tape, stick transfer paper over the surface where you want to transfer the design. Place the photocopied design on top, tape in place, and trace over the outlines with a pencil. This will transfer the design in a pale water-based ink which you can then paint over. Remove the paper and design.

3 Using a fine artist's brush and artist's acrylic paint, paint over the lines. Alternatively, if the design you want to transfer is not too intricate, you can copy elements of the design onto the surface freehand. Don't worry about wobbly lines—they add to the charm of hand-painted decoration. Allow the paint to dry, then apply two coats of varnish.

EXPERT TIPS

• *It is important when painting decoration onto a painted surface to remember to use water-based paint (or artist's acrylic paint) on a surface painted in water-based paint, and oil-based paint (satin or artist's oil paint) on a surface painted in semi gloss or satin paint.*

• *Elements of the curtain fabric could be echoed in other areas of the kitchen. For example, some shapes could be transferred onto the doors or onto the grey wooden floor.*

Making curtains from remnants

The fabric used for this project is original 1950s curtain material. The hem was unpicked, the curtain tape removed from the top and the fabric washed and ironed in preparation for alteration. The fabric is a wonderful example of the colours and pattern of its time: deep bright red, acid mustard, cream and pale grey are typical of the range of colours used in 1950s design. In fact, the fabric was so striking that the whole 1950s kitchen was based around its colours and design.

There are many wonderful and creative ways to make curtains—it is an art in itself. In this project, however, only the most simple of layman's methods are featured—sewing down the top and then using an iron-on hem webbing for the base—making the project quick and easy for beginners to tackle.

1 Measure the window drop and the width of the window to calculate the amount of fabric required. Generally, the fabric needs to be the length of the drop, plus 12.5 cm (5 in) for turning under and hemming, and one and a half times the width. Mark the lengths of fabric with tailor's chalk and cut as necessary.

2 Turn under the top edge of the curtain and iron the turn following the chalk mark. This will keep it even and straight for sewing later.

3 Using a sewing machine and matching thread, stitch the ironed section down in as straight a line as possible, leaving a channel through which to thread a curtain wire.

4 Place the iron-on hem webbing inside the creased and ironed hem so it is completely covered. Cover it with a damp cloth and press firmly with a hot dry iron. Hold the pressure for about 10 seconds until the cloth is dry and then repeat along the length of the hem. This will secure the hem in place. Thread a curtain wire through the top of the curtain and secure the ends onto screw eyes fixed on either side of the window.

EXPERT TIPS

• *This type of curtain is to hang decoratively at a window. If you want to be able to draw back the curtains more easily, attach a standard 2 cm (¾ in) curtain heading tape to the top of the curtain, and hang it from a rail.*

• *If you do not possess a sewing machine, you could sew the top hem by hand with a hem stitch that does not show through to the front of the curtain. For small kitchen curtains such as these, this need not be such a daunting task!*

67

Changing handles on kitchen units

Changing the knobs and handles on kitchen doors and drawers can transform their character. The 1950s style D-shaped handles are an integral part of this kitchen. With painted kitchens, it is particularly appropriate to change door and drawer handles. Old screw holes can be filled, sanded and painted over as if they had never been there, and new holes can then be drilled and new handles and knobs fitted. There is a wide variety of cupboard door furniture available, ranging from metal knobs and bars to coloured handles and wooden knobs. Although unfinished wood can be painted easily; varnished wood has to be prepared properly.

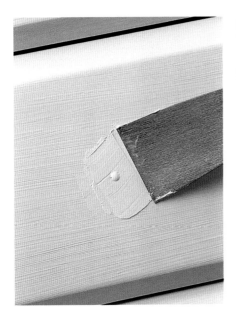

1 Remove the original drawer knobs, then fill the resulting screw holes with all-purpose filler. As the filler dries, it sinks into the hole, so it is best to fill with a slightly raised application. Leave to dry, then rub down the filler with sandpaper to make a flat smooth finish.

2 Measure the height and width of each drawer or door front and work out exactly where the new screw holes should be. Mark these positions lightly with a pencil.

3 Make sure you have the correct drill bit for your screws, then drill a clean straight hole at each of the marked points. Repeat for every drawer and door.

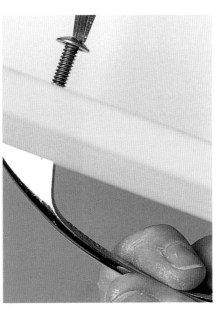

4 Prime the drawers and doors, then, when dry, paint them in the desired colour. Leave to dry, then seal with a coat of acrylic clear varnish. If any paint sticks in the screw holes, poke it out carefully when dry with a screw.

5 Attach the new handles by screwing them in place from the inside of the drawers and doors.

EXPERT TIPS

• *Remember that knobs and handles do not have to be placed in a central fashion. Experiment first by turning the handles horizontally, vertically, or placing them to the centre of the edge of the door rather than at the top. For some styles, two knobs on a drawer may be preferred. Check the effect by sticking the knobs and handles on with adhesive putty before drilling.*

M A K E O V E R   P R O J E C T

Lime Green

This contemporary kitchen makeover, decorated in varying shades of lime green and accented with stainless steel kitchen accessories, looks clean, fresh, practical and very vibrant.

Limes are an obvious inspiration for this colour scheme; inspiration is also found in young spring flowers and plants. Green is a colour associated with freshness and health, and is therefore highly appropriate for a kitchen. Stainless steel is a practical kitchen material, functional and clean, and it teams up well with lime green.

PROJECTS FROM THIS
MAKEOVER SHOW YOU

- HOW TO PAINT A
  CUPBOARD

- HOW TO FIT METAL
  GAUZE TO A CUPBOARD

- HOW TO PAINT A
  STORAGE BOX

- HOW TO PAINT A
  WINDOW FRAME

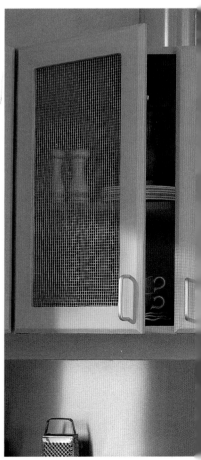

The unit doors were painted a deep strong lime green and then colourwashed and blended with a lighter shade to break up the colour, and create a gentler mottled effect. In keeping with the stainless steel accessories, new modern steel handles were fixed to the doors.

Steel sheets were then bought cut to size and glued to the wall to make a stylish splashback. This was sealed for protection.

The two glass doors on the kitchen cupboard were replaced by metal gauze. This can be bought at builders' merchants and cut to size with a pair of scissors. It is easy to fix the gauze to the doors (see page 75) and it completely changes their character. There are many different types of metal gauze suitable for this project. The main requirement is that it is stiff and strong and does not bend too easily. An alternative to metal gauze is perforated zinc, which was traditionally used to cover food before the days of refrigerators. The inside of the cupboard was painted deep violet. Used in small quantities, this vivid colour seems to break up the lime green well. It is always effective to paint inside cupboards with bright and lively colours but do make sure that the paint will adhere.

The walls were painted white, then washed in pale lime green; a darker shade was used for the back wall. Using the leftover paint, a few wooden storage boxes were painted in the two different lime greens, white and violet.

PAINTING A CUPBOARD

Painting a kitchen cupboard is straightforward if you pay attention to the little details. Careful masking is essential to avoid smearing an adjoining edge with paint, and using the right paintbrush can help you produce a professional and neat finish.

1 Before you begin painting, use masking tape to section off the worktop. Masking tape can be bought in varying widths. If the paint soaks into the wood it will be difficult to remove. Then, using a household brush, paint the cupboard door (see page 51).

2 Once the front of the cupboard door has been painted, open the door and paint the top edge of the cupboard if this is visible when the door is closed. Use a small fitch brush to paint into the corners and edges of the cupboard; a household brush might not cover the small surface evenly.

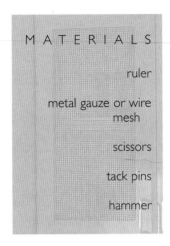

MATERIALS

ruler

metal gauze or wire
mesh

scissors

tack pins

hammer

Fitting a metal gauze door

This project is not as difficult as it seems—taking the glass out of the cupboard is probably the hardest part—and it completely changes the character of the cupboard.

When choosing metal mesh to use, make sure it is coated and will not rust. You can usually take home samples of mesh to think about before finally choosing a design.

1 Take the cupboard door off its hinges and carefully remove the glass panel by loosening or removing the clips holding it in position. Work slowly and methodically all around the panel to avoid breaking the glass.

2 Turn the cupboard door face down. Measuring from the rebate of the door, calculate the size of metal gauze required; it will probably be the same size as the glass.

EXPERT TIPS
- *Some types of metal mesh are available only in light or dull colours. If desired, paint the mesh with spray paint in a more appropriate colour.*

- *If the glass in your cupboard doors has been attached in a different way, use the instructions on this page as guidelines only.*

- *There is a great variety of woven mesh available. However, not all mesh is as easy to cut as the metal gauze featured here. You may have to ask a specialist supplier to cut it for you.*

3 Using a pair of household scissors, cut the metal gauze to the required size to fit the door. Check that it fits in the rebate at the back of the door.

4 Carefully lay the piece of metal gauze in the rebate of the door. Secure it in place with tack pins, hammering them in gently at 5 cm (2 in) intervals all around the rebate. These will not be visible from the front. Rehang the door on the cupboard to finish.

Painting a storage box

Unfinished pine storage boxes are ideal for painting and using up any leftover paint. As they are made from unfinished wood, water-based paints can be painted straight onto the surface and then sealed with an acrylic-based varnish. The darker lime colour on the box is the same colour that was used on the kitchen units; white was added to this to make the paler lime colour. The surround of the box is painted violet to contrast with the lime.

Storage boxes could be painted in numerous ways to fit in with a particular style of kitchen. For example, they could be painted in the bright distressed colours of the Caribbean kitchen, the soft floral patterns of the blue kitchen or even in an intricate pattern in browns and terracotta for the Moroccan-style kitchen.

1 Lightly rub the storage box with fine-grade sandpaper, sanding always in the direction of the wood grain. This will soften any hard edges of the wood, take off any splinters and smooth out any rough areas.

2 Remove the individual drawers and paint them separately with lime green. Paint a little into the edge of each drawer so that from the front the colour looks even. If desired, you could paint alternating drawers in pale lime, made by mixing a little white into the lime. Leave to dry.

EXPERT TIPS

• *Check that no paint or varnish settles in the U-shaped opening on the drawer fronts as this could later start to run and spoil the painted finish.*

• *If there are any knots in your new wooden items, seal them with knotting solution to prevent resin bleeding through (see step 3, page 45).*

3 Paint the frame of the storage box with violet water-based paint, going over the horizontal bands to cover the inside edges. Finish brushing in the direction of the wood grain. Allow to dry, sand down lightly, then apply a second coat and leave to dry.

4 Once the paint has dried out completely, apply a couple of coats of dead flat matt acrylic varnish over the frame and the drawers, allowing the first coat to dry before applying the second. This will make the storage box wipeable and waterproof, ideal for the kitchen.

all-purpose filler

filling knife

sandpaper

dusting brush

primer or undercoat

household brush

water-based paint

lining fitch

window scraper,
optional

Painting a window frame

There are ways of making window frame painting an easier task; the right tools and equipment can help tremendously. This window frame has been painted in lime green, the same colour as the kitchen units; too often woodwork is left white and not brought into the kitchen. As with most aspects of decorating, preparation is very important and the first steps of filling holes, rubbing down and undercoating are vital for achieving a good quality top coat. The same methods employed here can also be used on other woodwork, such as door and window architraves and skirting boards.

EXPERT TIPS

• *Using a window scraper is preferable to masking off the window as many tapes will leave a residue on the glass that cannot be scratched off and is difficult to remove.*

• *Paint a window frame early on a fine day so that it can dry during the day. Try to avoid closing a newly painted window before the paint has dried as this could cause the window to stick and the paintwork to spoil.*

1 Fill any holes in the window frame using all-purpose filler. Rub the surface well with sandpaper to achieve a smooth finish, then use a dusting brush or a dry soft brush to prepare a clean dust-free surface.

2 If your window frame is new wood, apply a coat of primer. If the frame is old and heavily repaired, apply undercoat. Many undercoat primers are now available as one product. Apply the primer or undercoat as smoothly as possible as this will affect the quality of the top coat. Leave to dry, then sand lightly and dust it as before.

3 Apply the top coat of water-based paint, using a lining fitch (a brush that has an angled head) to aid the cutting in of paint around the glass and where the frame meets the wall. Using a good quality brush will improve the finish.

4 When dry, use a window scraper to remove any paint that has splashed onto the glass. The smooth blade of a window scraper will scratch off paint without scratching or damaging the glass in any way.

MAKEOVER PROJECT

Sunny Caribbean

This vibrant-coloured kitchen with its bright turquoise, sunshine yellow and hot pink decor uses colours of the Caribbean to create a lively happy environment.

For inspiration in choosing bright and cheerful colours for your kitchen, look at exotic flowers, bright fabrics and patterns, food products and packages from the West Indies. In recent years, these colours have become more popular for use in interior decoration. Most paint companies now stock a range of suitable paint colours of this kind.

PROJECTS FROM THIS
MAKEOVER SHOW YOU

- HOW TO COLOURWASH
  A SURFACE

- HOW TO AGE A PAINTED
  SURFACE

- HOW TO CRACKLE GLAZE
  AND PAINT TERRACOTTA
  POTS

- HOW TO DECORATE
  GLASSWARE

Although strong and exceptionally vibrant, these colours are enjoyed in a Caribbean climate under the bright West Indian sunlight. In Europe, however, especially in certain houses, they may appear too harsh and strong. This is where ageing techniques can be used to good effect. The colours can be broken and softened considerably with antique washes and other ageing and broken colour effects.

On the kitchen doors, a bright turquoise was applied to a brown base that shows through in places where the paint has been chipped off. This effect was achieved by applying lumps of beeswax over the surface; once dry, turquoise water-based paint was used over the top and the beeswax scraped off with a filling knife to reveal patches of the brown base colour beneath (see page 31). This paint effect also creates the impression of age and wear. A wash of burnt umber was applied over the turquoise to age and soften the colour. The wooden door knobs were painted to match. The walls were colourwashed in a sunshine yellow water-based paint on top of a white base. The shutters, chairs and table legs were painted in the same way as the doors with bright pink water-based paint on top of a dark brown base coat.

The dark brown base colour used on the doors and shutters is evident in the floor. This dark floor contrasts with the vibrant colours used in the kitchen and holds the decorating scheme together.

COLOURWASHING A SURFACE

Colourwashing is a technique for achieving a mottled broken colour effect on a surface. For this project water-based paint and acrylic scumble glaze were used. The wash was applied over a base coat of white water-based paint. The surface should be well covered and even with no visible cracks, as imperfections will tend to show up more once the wash is applied. To create a more subtle, gentler effect, go over the walls with a second wash once the first is dry.

1 Prepare the glaze by mixing water-based paint with acrylic scumble glaze, adding more paint as desired. Brush the prepared glaze over the surface in all directions, tapering off at the edges.

2 Without leaving the glaze to dry, soften the glaze with a dusting brush. Brush over the glaze to soften the brushmarks and create a hazy cloudy finish.

EXPERT TIPS

• *An alternative way of colourwashing is to brush on the glaze as before, then wipe it off and rub it in with a soft cloth rather than a brush in certain areas. This creates a patchier, rougher-looking finish.*

• *You can use acrylic colourizers instead of water-based paint for a more transparent look. A more controlled application would be achieved on a less porous surface, such as low sheen or acrylic satin.*

Ageing a painted surface

In this project, a bright turquoise cupboard door is toned down and softened considerably by a simple ageing technique using artist's acrylic paint. This technique allows bright colours to be used in a decorating scheme without them dominating the room.

MATERIALS

acrylic clear varnish

burnt umber artist's acrylic paint

household brush

dusting brush

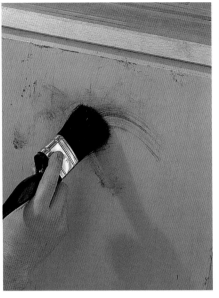

1 Place a spoonful of acrylic clear varnish on a piece of wood or old plate, then squirt a blob of burnt umber artist's acrylic paint next to it. Using a household brush, dab the tips of the bristles first in the varnish, then in the paint, touching only the tiniest spot of paint first—you can always add more to it.

2 Brush this mixture onto the surface of the door in an uneven way, spreading the colour wherever you want it to be. For an aged appearance that looks authentic, apply more colour where dirt and grime would usually collect, such as around the edges of the door or around the door knob.

3 Before the varnish and paint mixture has dried, go over any brushmarks that are visible on the surface with a dusting brush. This will produce a softer, more blended finish.

EXPERT TIP

• *If the varnish becomes tacky and is not softening and blending, wipe the varnish and artist's acrylic paint off the door quickly using a wet cloth. Once the door has been wiped clean and is dry, repeat the technique in the same way but using acrylic scumble glaze instead of acrylic varnish. The scumble glaze will not dry as quickly, allowing you more time to work with it. You will, however, have to wait longer for this to dry before you can apply acrylic clear varnish for protection.*

Glazing terracotta pots

MATERIALS

terracotta pot

blue water-based paint

household brush

crackle glaze

yellow water-based paint

artist's brush

dead flat acrylic varnish

As terracotta is an absorbent porous surface, water-based paint can be painted straight onto it. The bold colours used throughout the kitchen have been used again to jazz up these terracotta pots. The crackle glazed effect is an easy and fun way to use strong colours together—the red under the pink and the blue under the bright yellow, for example. It also creates an impression of age. The same effect was used on the units of the blue kitchen (see page 32). As water-based paint dries quickly, it can always be re-painted in a different colour if you are not happy with the final look. Once the pots are varnished, they will be wipeable and hardwearing.

1 Apply a base coat of water-based paint in your chosen base colour. Allow to dry and apply a second coat. The cracks will appear in the direction you apply the paint.

2 Once the base coat is dry, apply the crackle glaze in the same direction as the base coat. For strong cracks, as shown here, allow the first coat of glaze to dry out completely, then apply a second coat.

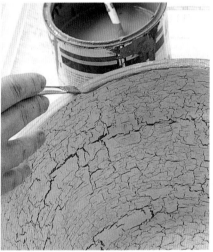

3 Once the crackle glaze has completely dried, apply the top coat of water-based paint in a contrasting colour in the same direction as before. Apply the paint in one sweeping motion and do not go over an area that has just been painted—this will pull the glaze off and ruin the effect. If this does happen, let it dry, then start again. Use enough paint just to cover the area. Allow to dry, when large cracks will appear.

4 Line the rim of the pot once the inside and outside are dry: apply a new base coat, then a coat of glaze, and then the top coat. Use a small artist's brush to create an even finish. Leave the pot to dry completely, then apply two coats of dead flat acrylic varnish over the pot to make it waterproof and wipeable.

Painting glassware

Painting glasses can add a splash of extra colour to your kitchen, and is both decorative and practical. There is a variety of glass paints available, all of which are suitable for different purposes, so take care to check the instructions and follow them carefully. Some paints create a matt and opaque finish while others give a semi transparent or glossy look. Some glass paint is for decorative use only and will come off easily if washed, while other brands can be left to cure for 24 hours before being baked in the oven and set. Some paints are safe when in contact with food and drink, but check with the manufacturer. It is easy to experiment with glass paints as most will wash off under running water before they have had time to set. Glass paints are available from most hobby and craft shops.

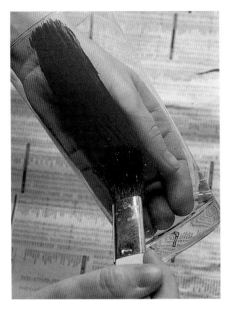

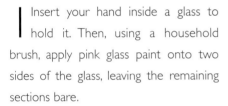

1 Insert your hand inside a glass to hold it. Then, using a household brush, apply pink glass paint onto two sides of the glass, leaving the remaining sections bare.

2 Before the paint starts to dry, drag the paint evenly down the sides of the glass with a clean dry brush to create a dragged effect. If you do not achieve a clean edge, wipe off any excess paint with a damp cloth.

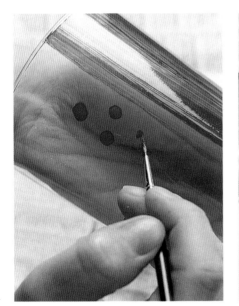

3 Holding the glass flat, paint pink dots on the clear sections of the glass with a small brush. For greater definition, you may have to go over them a second time. Do not apply too much paint at once as it could run.

4 Using a fine artist's brush, paint the rim of the glass in the same colour for added definition. The base of the glass can also be painted, if desired. Some glass paints require baking to set; always follow the manufacturer's instructions regarding oven temperatures as they can vary.

Brushes

BADGER SOFTENER
This brush is made from very soft, long bristles of pure badger hair. Use it to tickle away brushstrokes from wet glazes and to give an out-of-focus appearance. It is essential for marbling work and useful in creating a colourwash effect. Meticulous cleaning is important as badger brushes are very expensive to replace. Condition them with hair conditioner regularly.

ARTIST'S FITCHES
Usually made from hog's hair and quite stiff, fitches are invaluable as detailing brushes and for mixing smaller quantities of paint. Cheap fitches are fine, unless you are using them for mural work, in which case better quality brushes will give a more even brushstroke. The bristles of good-quality fitches are slightly curved in towards the top of the brush.

FINE ARTIST'S BRUSHES
For detailing and fine mural work, a selection of medium-quality fine artist's brushes is important. Imitation sable or nylon work well and are less expensive than real sable or pony hair brushes. Store them in a tube or brush wrap; do not store soft brushes in a pot with the bristles pointing downwards as they will bend.

DUSTING BRUSH
This has endless uses, from dusting items before painting, to colourwashing and dragging. Natural bristle is more flexible and durable.

DRAGGING BRUSH
This is a speciality brush with extra long flexible bristles for creating a fine striped effect. If you have a choice of dragging brush, always go for one with a comfortable handle.

FLOGGER
This brush has extremely long, floppy bristles which, when gently tapped into wet glaze, create the distinctive flecks seen in natural woodgrains.

VARNISHING BRUSH

Not essential but such a joy to work with, a varnishing brush is only about 5 mm (¼ in) thick. The bristles are very flexible, hold a lot of varnish or paint and help to feather oil-based paints in particular so that a perfectly smooth paint surface is obtained with minimum effort.

SASH BRUSHES

Originally designed to help with the painting of complicated sash windows, sash brushes are available with pointed or rounded tips. They are perfect for edging and lining, and also for stippling paint on small areas or when control is required. With a little practice you will be able to apply paint in a perfectly straight line by using a sash brush. It may well become an essential part of your decorating kit and reduce your masking tape expenses.

STIPPLING BRUSH

Use a stippling brush for removing brushstrokes and for creating a dotty stippled paint effect. Most decorators use stippling brushes about 5 cm (2 in) square. Larger stipplers are faster to work with but become heavy as the hours pass. Stippling brushes are expensive and can be replaced at a push with a large paint brush from which the loose bristles have been carefully picked out. If you use a paint brush be sure to move it around as you work in order to avoid the imprint of the straight edges showing.

HOUSEHOLD BRUSHES

A good selection of general household brushes is the starting point for any decorator. Buy the most expensive you can afford; cheap brushes will shed many hairs and not last long. Look out for a hole in the middle of the bristles which has been filled with a wooden wedge. This will fill with paint and the brush will drip.

WALLPAPER PASTING BRUSH

Use this large brush for smoothing wallpaper into position on a wall. It is wide and comfortable to handle for long periods at a time.

Tools

ROLLERS

Use long-pile rollers for textured finishes or uneven surfaces, and short-pile rollers for a smooth finish. A foam roller is useful for a smooth finish with oil-based paints but may bubble or 'orange peel'; work slowly with a well-loaded roller to avoid this. The small rollers sold for gloss paint are a useful addition to any painter's kit as they can be cleaned more easily than larger rollers.

SANDPAPER

Available in different grades, sandpaper is used for rubbing down and smoothing surfaces prior to painting, and for cleaning.

ICE CUBE TRAY

Useful as a palette that holds a little sample of many colours at one time; it is easy to hold in one hand at the top of a ladder when painting detailing and murals.

PAINT PADS

These are wonderful speed painters, faster than a brush and smoother than a pile roller. Made from foam with a mohair painting surface, they are available in a wide range of sizes. Paint pads are more economical with paint and much easier to wash than rollers. Work in every direction adjusting the pressure from light to heavy as the pad runs out of paint.

TACK RAGS

These are sold as disposable cloths on a roll, or separately packed. They are lightly impregnated with spirits and oils and are perfect for wiping away dust after sanding a wooden item, prior to priming, painting and varnishing it. The oils and spirits can also help with cleaning paintwork prior to painting but sugar soap should be used for vigorous cleaning.

TOOLS FOR GLAZE WORK

Not all glaze finishes are carried out with the aid of an expensive speciality brush. Plastic bags can be screwed up and used to create a leathery effect, sponges can be used for various effects and rags used to create a soft mottled look. Experiment with anything that will not leave lint or fluff in the glaze.

PAINT TRAYS

These are not just for rolling paint, they are also useful for standing open cans of paint in and for mixing small quantities of paint.

DISPOSABLE PAPER PALETTE

Use this for tiny quantities of several colours at one time. The tear-off sheets eliminate any cleaning at the end of the day. Very comfortable to hold for long periods.

PAINT KETTLES

Sturdy and reliable containers for a tin of paint or a glaze mixture. A kettle can be hung from the top of a ladder with a meat hook or the handle. Keep an empty kettle handy for putting wet brushes in. Plastic kettles need not be washed after use and can be re-used after the paint has dried until eventually you throw them away.

MAHL STICK

This is a cane with a soft ball of chamois leather or cloth tied to the end. For high work that requires a very steady hand, hold the mahl stick in your non-painting hand, supporting the cane under your arm. Rest the ball on the wall. You can then rest your painting wrist on the stick and remain steady, even for minute details. If required you can make a mahl stick by attaching a cut tennis ball to one end of a cane with a large square of chamois leather wrapped over the ball and tied securely to the cane.

Suppliers & Acknowledgements

Dulux Australia
Stockists of Dulux, Berger,
Walpamur and British Paints
in a huge range of colours.
Contact 13 2525 (national
toll-free number).

Haymes Paints
25 Scott Parade
Ballarat Vic. 3350
Tel: (03) 5332 1234
Painted finishes supplies.

Langridge Artists' Colours
120 Langridge Street
Collingwood Vic. 3066
Tel: (03) 9419 4453
Artist's supplies.

Oxford Art Supplies
221–223 Oxford Street
Darlinghurst NSW 2011
Tel: (02) 9360 4066
Artist's supplies.

Porter's Original Paints
592 Willoughby Rd
Willoughby NSW 2068
Tel: (02) 9958 0753
Household paints, scumble
glaze, crackle glaze and acrylic
clear varnishes.

The publishers wish to thank the following photographers and organizations for their kind permission to reproduce the photographs in this book on the following pages: p.6 (top) Paul Ryan / International Interiors; p.6 (bottom) James Merrell / Homes & Gardens / Robert Harding; p.7 (top) Simon Kenny / Belle / Courtesy of Porters Paints Australia / Arcaid; p.7 (bottom) and p.15 James Merrell / Options / Robert Harding; p.12 Cecilia Innes / The Interior Archive; p.14 Ian Skelton / Homes & Ideas / Robert Harding

Index

Dedication

With love to my mother, Mary

Acknowledgements

A million thank yous: to Dai Williams for taking most of the photographs, with unlimited generosity and wholeheartedness; to Clare Hunt for such beautiful styling; to Kris Watson for his most beautiful set building—and palaver; to Simon Whitmore for his very kind studio assistance and impromptu hand modelling; and to Dominic Blackmore for taking the extra pictures so sweetly. Thank you to everyone involved in this project and all at Merehurst, especially Sara Colledge, Sarah Duffin and Anna Sanderson for taking over and managing us all so calmly and kindly.

Published by Murdoch Books®, a division of Murdoch Magazines Pty Ltd, 45 Jones Street, Ultimo NSW 2007

This edition published 1999. First published in 1999 by Merehurst Limited. Copyright © 1999 Merehurst Limited

National Library of Australia Cataloguing-in-Publication Data.
Cummings, Catherine. Kitchen makeover & project book. Includes index.
ISBN 0 86411 810 4. 1. Kitchens - Remodeling. 2. Interior decoration. I. Title.
II. Title: Better homes and gardens (North Sydney, N.S.W.). 747.797

Editor: Heather Dewhurst

Designers: Siân Keogh and Martin Laurie at Axis Design

Photographer: Dai Williams and Dominic Blackmore

Stylist: Clare Hunt

Series concept and Creative Director: Marylouise Brammer

Commissioning Editor: Anna Sanderson

CEO & Publisher: Anne Wilson

International Sales Director: Mark Newman

Colour separation by Bright Arts in Hong Kong

Printed in Queensland by Prestige Litho

PRINTED IN AUSTRALIA